Enveloped

CW01502254

Enveloped

Amy Phillips

The Pentland Press Limited
Edinburgh • Cambridge • Durham • USA

1-99

First published in 1999 by
The Pentland Press Ltd.
1 Hutton Close
South Church
Bishop Auckland
Durham

British Library Cataloguing in Publication Data.
A Catalogue record for this book is available
from the British Library.

ISBN 1 85821 729 6

Typeset by CBS, Martlesham Heath, Ipswich, Suffolk
Printed and bound by Antony Rowe Ltd., Chippenham

By the same author:

Tincture (a collection of work)
published by Paper Doll. 1999.

To all those who have touched my life over the years, from Felixstowe to Derby, Keswick, Penrith, Dukes Priory and back again, you know who you are.

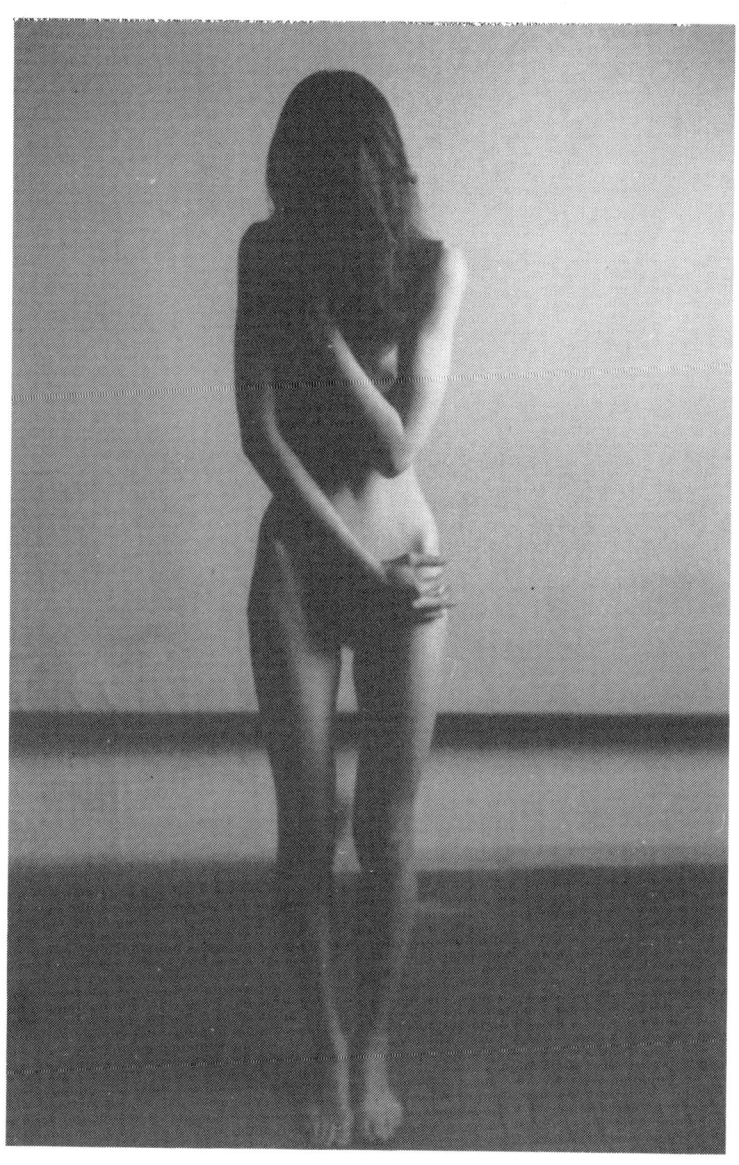

Photographed by Heidi Cable

Preface

This book chronicles the last five years pieced together from the diaries I kept during what has been an almost indescribable time, one that fades from the memory, as so often I forgot. Without these diaries I would have very little recollection of this period of my life.

Re-reading the entries brings it all back, the feelings, the sensations of panic, the fear and how I thought I'd never be free.

It's a journey through an anorexic existence, through a disintegration of self to near death and deep depression and finally a recovery, not least a discovery of the factors beyond my control which accumulated to cause illness.

Looking back I am often amazed I survived and wonder how I had the strength to fight on. Despite the bleakness there is hope within these words. I write this not as an exploitation of experience for the voyeuristic, nor as an explanation for my actions but rather as a testament, as a truth, for without these experiences I am nothing.

Foreword by a Friend

Understanding other people's despair is so frustrating, especially when you can not understand why they do not understand the remedy: try convincing someone suffering from anorexia that they are truly beautiful, and you'll be banging your head against a wall in minutes.

What makes Amy's work in this volume so compelling is her insight and understanding of the six years she suffered from food disorders, knowing in her own self that she wasn't 'anorexic', even though told otherwise. And whilst she experienced all the psychological and physical symptoms, indulged in bingeing and faced near starvation, mental breakdown and body disfunction, she was convinced there was another reason, and she was proved right.

From childhood she had experienced recurring abdominal pain, and in puberty knew she was intolerant to much of what she ate. When I first met her some twelve years ago she had arrived at Deben High School in Felixstowe as just another student, very slim, very pretty and very intelligent. I now learn she kept most of her health and psychological anxieties hidden: she'll today admit to feeling isolated then, being different, and suffering at the hands of those who take advantage of others in any school system. By the age of eighteen she was still slim, very beautiful and destined for success in whichever of the arts she wished that she excelled in. Few of us who had contact with her knew of any problems, and similarly few of us questioned that she had everything going for her. Her diaries begin at about that time.

I met her again five years later, last year, and she had recently published 'Tincture', a small volume of poetry that had somehow restored her sense of self. She had been through five years of hell, for the sake of a better cliché, and had managed to document the experience, largely because she knew that 'anorexia' wasn't her problem, yet she suffered all the nightmare of the anorexic. She had in fact gone on to study art, hence a lot of the photography contained in this book. Nude photographs may strike the reader as a contradiction, but they should remind the reader of her intelligence and objectivity. Her writing has so much immediacy, and honesty, and all the time you are conscious of the battle taking place, and the courage needed to face it. Yes, there are loose ends, intrusive characters, and gaps, but again, they reflect the stream of her conscious living.

How many are there of those who yearn for the waif-model appearance, and who fall into the anorexia trap? How many are there, similarly afflicted, and yet remaining misdiagnosed? Amy now has to be so careful of her diet: endless foods that most of us take for granted create an adverse reaction. And five years of not knowing have left her with medical problems that have yet to be fully resolved: irritable bowel syndrome, candida albicans (yeast overgrowth), amenorrhoea (lack of periods), and a high risk of osteoporosis.

I hope this book is read by so many who should be aware of the individual, not least the thousands who work in both health and education, and the many thousands who suffer similarly: they should all gain much.

D.M.

Enveloped

In the beginning, well not really . . . Felixstowe (1993)

I was diagnosed as anorexic, 20th December, 1993. I didn't see myself as anorexic. My image of an anorexic is of somebody deliberately starving themself, thinking they're fat. I didn't think like that. I felt sort of ashamed, I guess, because I've let myself get this way. I'm glad Mum came with me because otherwise I don't think I would have been able to cope with the way he launched into me. He weighed me and I was six stone and six pounds, which I was quite pleased with considering that at one stage my weight had dropped to barely six stone. It meant my plan of action had started to work. But no, he was a bit shocked and after examining me commented that I looked like something out of Belsen.

'Are you eating?'

'Do you make yourself sick afterwards?'

'Could you have AIDS? No, you look too healthy to be an AIDS case.'

So now I'm being referred to somebody at the hospital who'll, I don't know, give me counselling of some sort I guess. I'm just waiting for an appointment.

I understand his diagnosis. It's based on the fact I've lost a lot of weight (two stone in six months), a lack of periods, which stopped in March (I came off the Pill, had one cycle and not a drop since), and because there is no other known illness to account for the weight loss. So, there you go, I'm supposed to have Anorexia Nervosa: but it's strange . . . whilst I know it's an illness, and the symptoms are mental rather than physical, I tend to forget there's anything wrong.

It wasn't until the end of November that I realised just how rapidly I was losing weight. At the beginning of September I was levelling off at seven stone, but by November I was barely six stone. That was when I decided to do some nude portraits to

1

show myself how thin I had become, which was quite an emotionally draining experience. In a perverse way I was pleased with the results, but at the same time I felt sick at myself because some of the images are quite horrific, disturbing. I still find some of them difficult to look at. From November on I decided I needed to seriously make an effort to regain the lost weight.

I've been given a hospital appointment for February 1994 to see a consultant of some kind. In the meantime it's left up to me to try and sort myself out. I even had some counselling which didn't really work, and have read up about anorexia in an attempt to understand.

The report from the consultant back to the doctor confirms he doesn't consider me to be suffering from Anorexia Nervosa.

I am so pissed off with my doctor, just to say I'm anorexic. He didn't bother to find out if anything else was causing it. He really is just so . . . he didn't listen to me. IBS (Irritable Bowel Syndrome) now seems to be the problem. Colofac has been prescribed, which does bugger all and leaves me feeling so ill. Last Friday I saw the doctor: he said I was obviously suffering from depression and tried to put me on anti-depressants. I said, no way. His reply was that until I tried them he couldn't do anything else for me. Well, thank you! God, he makes me so fucking angry. I'm bound to feel upset if I spend most of my time unwell. He says it's depression and stress. I say it's food intolerance that keeps setting off the IBS, but he won't listen. NO, so it's down to me to sort this out by mixing my food about: oranges and apples are things to avoid.

It gets difficult to gain weight when you feel this bad: gas, nausea, pounding headaches, feverish, visual disturbances and dizziness. I also feel fatigued with aches, pains in the knees, pains inside the back (kidney area) and a constant thirst. No appetite. Eating aggravates and prolongs the discomfort.

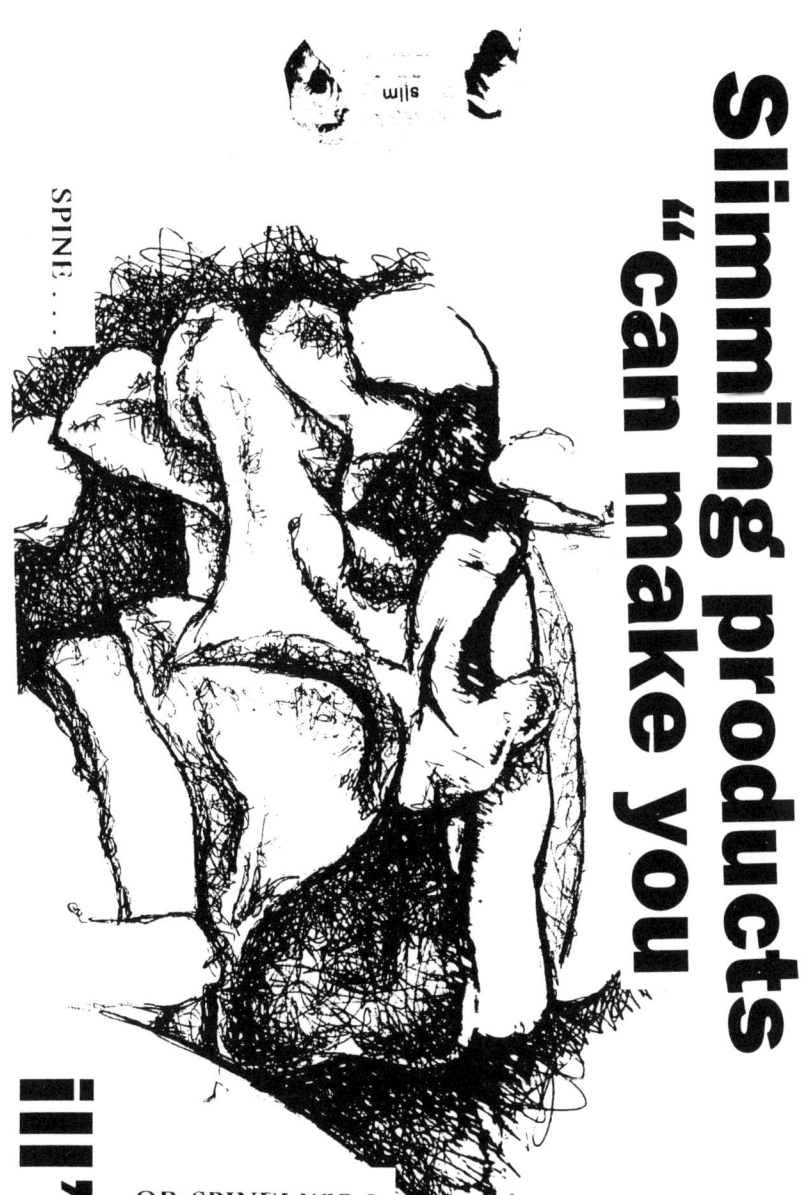

Slimming products "can make you

ill"

SPINE . . . .

Stuck inside this frail frame.
Take 2 steps forward, 2 steps back.

OR SPINELESS ?

3

1993

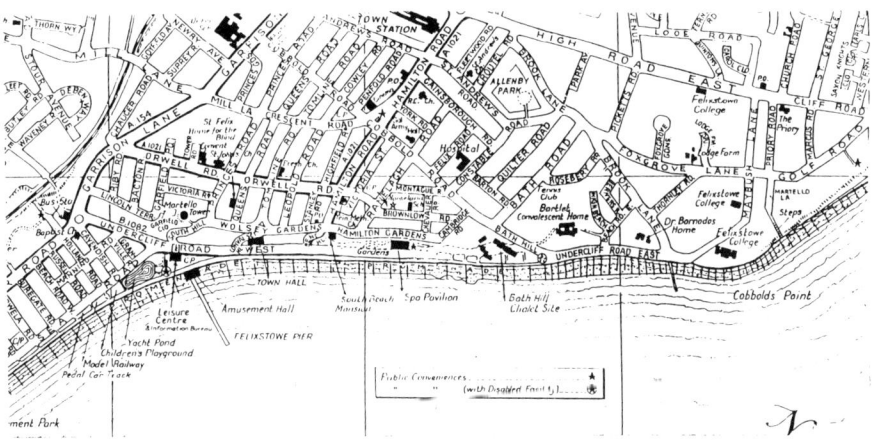

APRIL
Friday 9th April 1993 – Felixstowe
Had a major scare with our hamster, Dylan. We went to get him out of his cage and he was cold, stiff, barely moving, barely breathing and unable to open his eyes. He was all skin and bone. It was horrible: when I held him I was in tears. I sat there for an hour by the fire with him curled up in a tight little ball in my hands. We were convinced he was going to die. Eventually he began to respond to me. He took the odd peanut and began to stagger around.

Sunday 11th April 1993
He's improved so much, still thin though. I tried to sketch him but he kept running off!

JUNE
11th June 1993 – Brugge Bike Trip.
We've made it despite the odd hiccup. I'm now in the youth hostel, in a room with Jo, Anna and Kate, and at last I'm lying

7

down comfortably. At the moment the others have dropped off so all I can hear is the wind rushing through the trees.

The ferry crossing was OK. I was dreading it. I'm not keen on boats, so I drank. Didn't get much sleep, ended up balanced between two chairs, curled up in a tight ball trying to keep warm under my coat. To be honest I'm not feeling at all well, my stomach is not happy. I feel lifeless.

The room is white, pure, basic, closed in feeling: it makes me think of a room in a mental institution.

12th June 1993

It's 6pm and I'm starting to get tired now. It's raining again.

Got out of bed to cycle in search of some nightlife. The rain was hammering down and got soaked to the skin within minutes. We walked around for ages until eventually we came across the Cactus Cafe. I had one drink and then headed back, still wet, with Anna, stopping for chips on the way. Arrived back at midnight and had a gorgeous hot chocolate.

13th June 1993

Took a trip to Ghent. An excellent day.

Someone stole my passport from our room and we eventually found it planted in Emma's bag. Oh, ha ha. How amusing.

14th June 1993

One last trip into Brugge and got soaked. I've spent the last few days living on bread, cheese and chocolate. I'm really craving pasta sauce, pizza, a hot meal. Not that I mind bread and cheese but you can have too much of some things.

More wine on the crossing home. All in all I've had a really good time; it's given me the urge to travel. I think that because I haven't joined in much in the evenings etc, that people think I haven't enjoyed myself but in my own strange way, it's been great, done me a world of good. I feel so happy, relaxed, so much better than before, positive. I just feel like dancing about.

15th June 1993

My hamster's dead. I just burst into tears. It's typical, I leave him for a few days and he dies without me.

Recurring dream: I'm in a white room, people around, clinical, could be doctors, their faces, unrecognisable. They're forcibly injecting me with other people's memories, in the hand and the arm. I'm then transported back to the factory, the silver, mirrors and people. It was as though I was physically there but also being a detached observer. Strange and cool.

20th June 1993

I am haunted by the things that have been and by the things I will never see.
I am haunted by the things that I long for but can never have.
Deep inside the sleeping mind these desires seem to be reality.
I love those I know I can never have.
Actions, encounters and impossible embraces,
spoken words I long to hear,
unthinkable in the real world.
Lifted by happiness
then thrown into turmoil by these emotions.
Wanting only makes the hurt worse,
wanting becomes obsession,
perverse and cruel.

JULY

Monday 5th July 1993

Wandered to the beach at 1 p.m. Humid, odd breeze, sea murky brown and not much rubbish around, just the usual; burger carton floating in the waves, crisp bags, cigarette packets, the remains of sanitary towels along the shoreline, flies in the sand and stones. Couldn't get around Cobbold Point, tide too high. Sometimes the beach can be so nice, mainly in the evenings and early mornings, I find interesting stones, shells and objects washed up, plus there aren't people around.

Tuesday 6th July 1993
A nightmare involving a slaughter house.

Thursday 8th July 1993
Spent the day travelling to Cornwall to see Dad so I haven't had a chance to do much except watch the landscape zip by and think.

Friday 9th July 1993
Staying at a really nice B&B in Camelford; you can hear the river all through the night.

Monday 12th July 1993
Travelling back home. I've been thinking a lot about my Dad. It's hard only seeing him for a few days a year, I miss him so much. I've also thought a lot about Ros and the things we used to get up to. When I think about it, Cornwall, spending the summer there, seeing Ros when she came down, it was the only place I could truly be myself, not worry about sounding stupid or feeling inhibited by my lisp because there wasn't anybody there who'd put me down or make me feel small. I was free.

Friday 23rd July 1993
I've been having trouble sleeping lately so I've spent the time reading.

Enveloped

Saturday 24th July 1993

4.45 a.m. Haven't been able to sleep so I decided to take Chloe to the beach. Fresh, pure, the only sounds are those created by nature. Peaceful, lovely. A police car cruised by. Home at 6 a.m. and got 4 hours sleep.

Wednesday 28th July 1993

2.45 a.m. and once again I can't get to sleep. I feel tired but . . . I've also got a blood test later on which I'm not looking forward to.

AUGUST
4th August 1993

Didn't sleep very well last night and when I did I had a strange dream, all connected with Sartre's Age of Reason which I'm reading at the moment. It was like being at and in a movie, you could see the characters, the scenes, their conversations. I was in the place of Marcelle who had become pregnant by Matthew, needing money for an abortion and now he was considering marriage. I decided I wanted to keep the baby. I remember saying, 'these are two things I have always been against, having a baby and marriage.' So what has changed?

14th August 1993

Today I went on an Animal Rights march from Eye to Occold, to the Pharmco LSR building where they test on animals. It was a very moving and memorable experience.

24th August 1993

SEX on TV. Sex in films, in magazines. SEX OBSESSED SOCIETY. I can't get away from it: SEX, SEX, SEX. Are you getting enough? Does your man measure up? 101 ways to keep your sex life spicy. Latest sex survey. Tacky teen mags sell sex. Everywhere I turn: SEX. So why do I feel so SEXLESS?

SEPTEMBER
20th September 1993
Today I am twenty. Physically I don't look it but mentally I feel it. A day like any other except college has started. Since listening to BLUE last night I seem very aware of it today, everywhere. Blue cars, blue signs, blue shoes, blue door frames, blue flowers, so many shades creating a panorama.

21st September 1993
It's 3 a.m. I can't sleep. I need some sleep.

24th September 1993
It's the end of my first week back at college. How's it been? Well, I was raring to go, to get into my work but after the three day intro thing and being given projects to do, I now feel very stifled. I just want to do my own thing. I'm feeling quite down and exhausted. It's going to take a while to get used to getting up at 6.30 a.m., the horrible bus journey, the cold mornings and lugging my art box etc around. When I get home at night I'm just not capable of doing any work, all I want to do is go to bed. Things can only improve!

29th September 1993
Aaargh! I'm so tired, can't cope with doing any work. I was supposed to spend the day with Ian. The only chance I get to see him now and I end up having to come home by 2 p.m. and collapsing into bed for a few hours. I guess it must be a month or so since we stopped seeing each other. It seems strange, I still think of him as my boyfriend: it's a hard habit to break after

nearly four and a half years. It's for the best, I think, now we're purely best friends. I don't know why I haven't told you this before. We never argued, so . . . the reason I can't say here. All I can say is my illness and general lack of hormones doing what they should do contributed to it.

30th September 1993
Have listened to BLUE from start to finish. I am deeply moved and write this with tears slowly trickling down my cheeks.

OCTOBER
1st October 1993
End of my second week. It seems longer! Feeling ugh, tired, lifeless, can't seem to get on with my work even though I want to. End up in bed by 9.30 p.m. most nights, not sleeping well either.

3rd October 1993
STRESSED. I feel tired, lifeless, ideas aren't coming together. Frustrated. Can't produce work for the sake of it, there must be feeling/meaning behind it. I want to leave, I won't. Art is so important to me, my life revolves around it, sometimes it gets too much. I want to run away, need a change. I need love or just to be hugged. Insecure me.
On Saturday I screamed 'I WISH I WAS DEAD' and cried. On Sunday I cried.

NOVEMBER
Tuesday 2nd November 1993 – Amsterdam Trip
Ferry crossing long and boring. Finally got to the Hans Brinker hostel at about 10.30 p.m. Hungry and tired, went to bed, six to

a room, very basic and quite cold.

It's just gone midnight. I'm having some veggie soup, don't feel well, can't sleep.

Wednesday 3rd November 1993

Slept OK, bit cold though. Lovely brekkie. Never guess who I bumped into at breakfast, Matt. What a bizarre coincidence, to come all this way and he's staying in the same hostel!

Out all day, back at hostel for 6.30 p.m. I didn't bother to go out again, feeling really tired. Went to bed, couldn't sleep, too noisy.

Thursday 4th November 1993

Spent today generally wandering around. Walked up to Anne Frank's house but decided not to go in and instead sat on a bridge for an hour or so watching the canal and the water distorting the reflections.

Haven't sampled any of the food. I've been making sandwiches at breakfast to eat during the day.

Feeling very drained and tired, can't face going out tonight. I'm eating more than usual, thought it would perk me up but . . . My knees are so sore, must have covered quite a few miles today.

I can't believe we're going home tomorrow.

Friday 5th November 1993

Didn't sleep at all well, think that's the reason I've felt so tired all the time.

Monday 15th November 1993

Had a bizarre dream last night. In it I was giving birth. It didn't hurt at all (definitely a dream!). I remember looking down and seeing this head and body squeezing out of me.

Enveloped

Thursday 25th November 1993

Feeling emotionally drained but on such a high. Today with the help of Heidi, I was able to take my nude self portraits. Felt a bit nervous to begin with but I'm glad Heidi was there. We only had an hour to complete the session so it was quick and intense.

Friday 26th November 1993

I've taken the nude self portraits which show how thin I've become so it's now time for change. It's been nine months since I've had a period. Physically I need to make myself stronger. Lowest weight 6st 6lbs. I've lost nearly one and a half stone in eight months. I'm making a positive effort to put it back on. Need to gradually eat more, not crappy chocolate. The way to do this is eat more nutritious foods, beans, cheese and increase size of meals. I am aware of what's happening. I may have some mental hang up with food deep inside my mind but I am not anorexic. If I was I'd be denying the fact I've become so thin, instead I'm facing up to this.

DECEMBER

Friday 3rd December 1993

Weighed myself this morning, I've lost another two pounds. Can't really describe how I feel. Scared, upset, disappointed because I've really tried eating more yet still I'm losing weight. Emotionally I'm having a bad time, feel stressed, a lot on my mind, perhaps I'm pushing myself too hard. There seems to be so little time and so much I need to do. I never really stop working. I guess I could do with relaxing, actually going out for a change. What do I need? A friend.

I feel on the verge of crying, so tensed up, can't wait for the Xmas hols, time to relax, have a break. All my dashing around

15

Enveloped

Enveloped

Photographed by Heidi Cable

Enveloped

Enveloped

Photographed by Heidi Cable

at college is burning off the food as fast as I'm eating it.

31st December 1993

I binged for the first time last night and it has left me feeling extremely unwell today. Ugh. I crammed on sweet, sugary stuff and dough, then curled up tight in bed and tried to sleep the pain away.

Enveloped

Enveloped

1994

Enveloped

Enveloped

Photographed by Heidi Cable

25

Enveloped

Enveloped

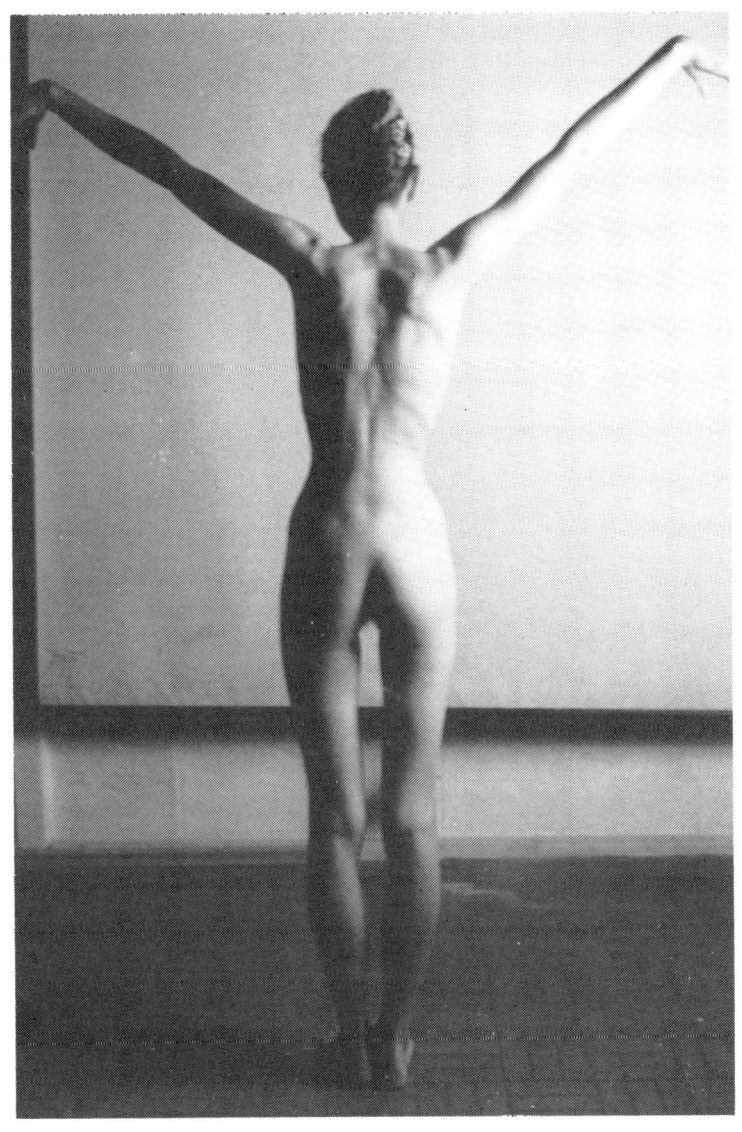

Photographed by Heidi Cable

Enveloped

FEBRUARY
11th February 1994
   Whitechapel: Bill Viola's Slowly Turning Narrative. Sounds, images merge. 'The one who infects, the one who . . .' again and again. I felt like screaming, almost hysterical, mesmerised. I felt as it built up that the screen would speed up and spin out of control.

18th February 1994
   I feel so low. I'm trying to produce work but I don't, it just isn't flowing. It's like everything I do doesn't seem right, lack of concentration I guess. I feel trapped, as if I'm pacing around this mental cell, unable to see any way out. So lifeless. I have the urge to get drunk, eat pizza and watch a film. Relax that is, but the more my work isn't working, the harder it is for me not to think about it.
   Oh hell.

25th February 1994
   I feel so happy today, just like dancing around. Awoke at 4 a.m., walked along the beach at 7 a.m. It was so gorgeous, fresh

and free. Am I finally sorting things out for the better?

APRIL
Monday 11th April 1994
   Excellent day, feeling bouncy, happy and confident. I feel so good mentally and physically.

Tuesday 12th April 1994
   Another good day – keeping busy.

Thursday 14th April 1994
   Generally feeling very tired, not like doing much but I had to go to London, National Theatre with Emma to see *The Skriker*. Play was excellent, Kathryn Hunter was stunning. Weather pretty crappy, not in the mood for wandering about, just fancied going home and into bed with a lovely bowl of hot soup. Reading the *Rachel Papers* – Martin Amis.
   Collapsed into bed totally exhausted.

Friday 15th April 1994
   Shitty weather. Had a call from Ian to see how I was and arranged to see him later. I'm feeling bouncy now. Lovely evening and perfect pizzas, watched the box. I have such a mass of confused emotions. I know I have enormous feelings for him, such care, but is it love? I'm not sure. I don't know how to tell any more. I think it's unlikely we'll get together again, it'd be strange. In fact if we'd still been seeing each other it would be 5 years today. I guess 4 odd years isn't bad for a relationship but I feel I will never have another one again which probably sounds silly but I can't imagine I'll ever meet anyone else who is remotely interested in me. Talk about low self esteem.

Enveloped

Saturday 16th April 1994

Woke up with a churning tum but generally feeling bouncy. Stomach got very tight after dinner (pizza) so I went up town to walk it down. Feeling very compulsive, kept going into shops and buying more food to eat even though I was in intense pain, then came home. Feeling very depressed, cuppa tea, more food. Took the dog out. Desperately feel like being sick, it'd relieve the feeling but I can't be.

Crying, feel so fed up. Scared at myself. Very strong compulsive urges that'll end up making me feel worse. Got on my bike and went for a demonic ride to try to blow the cobwebs out of my brain. Came back and laid down, felt calmer.

Nice evening meal of salad and Indian take-away, several glasses of wine, continued snacking, I know I shouldn't when I already feel this dodgy but I can't control it.

Sunday 17th April 1994

Stomach seriously churning. Ugh. In a very delicate state. Went for a drive, bit jumpy in places, not co-ordinating at all well. Feel as though I'm not really here, physically I am but mentally I'm elsewhere, can't concentrate on anything and feeling tired.

Wednesday 20th April 1994

Feeling very drained. Limbs heavy as if someone's sucked out all my energy.

Friday 22nd April 1994

Finally got the energy to have breakfast at 9 a.m. I should have gone in today but I feel so tired and the thought of the bus journey and running about sorting things out was too much. Instead spent the day knitting elastic samples.

Enveloped

Sunday 24th April 1994

Today has been so bad I don't even want to talk about it.

Monday 25th April 1994

Spent the day knitting webs out in the garden in my shorts! Lovely, relaxing. Hell, everything's coming to the surface, Mum's shocked at how thin I am, she's concerned. I'm upset. I've weighed myself and to be honest I've lost weight. Our scales read 6st 1lb: 6lbs has just gone. I need to sort my life out.

I need to change it which I can't do while I'm at college. At the moment I'm drifting, trapped in a state of non being and I'm scared of life. I just don't know what to do. Help me – PLEASE.

Scared. I lie in bed,
huddled up
arms wrapped tightly around my ribcage.
I can feel my bony ribs and backbone.
It frightens me
no control.

JUNE

SOLO, SO LOW, SOL ARE

I stand in a queue, basket full of food
and people they stare.
I feel their eyes scanning my scrawny frame.
I return their stares with hard, fixed eyes.
'What's your problem?'

I'd love to scream.

Sometimes I hear comments whispered as I pass.
I know what they think ANOREXIC.

Enveloped

Photographed by Heidi Cable

Enveloped

Enveloped

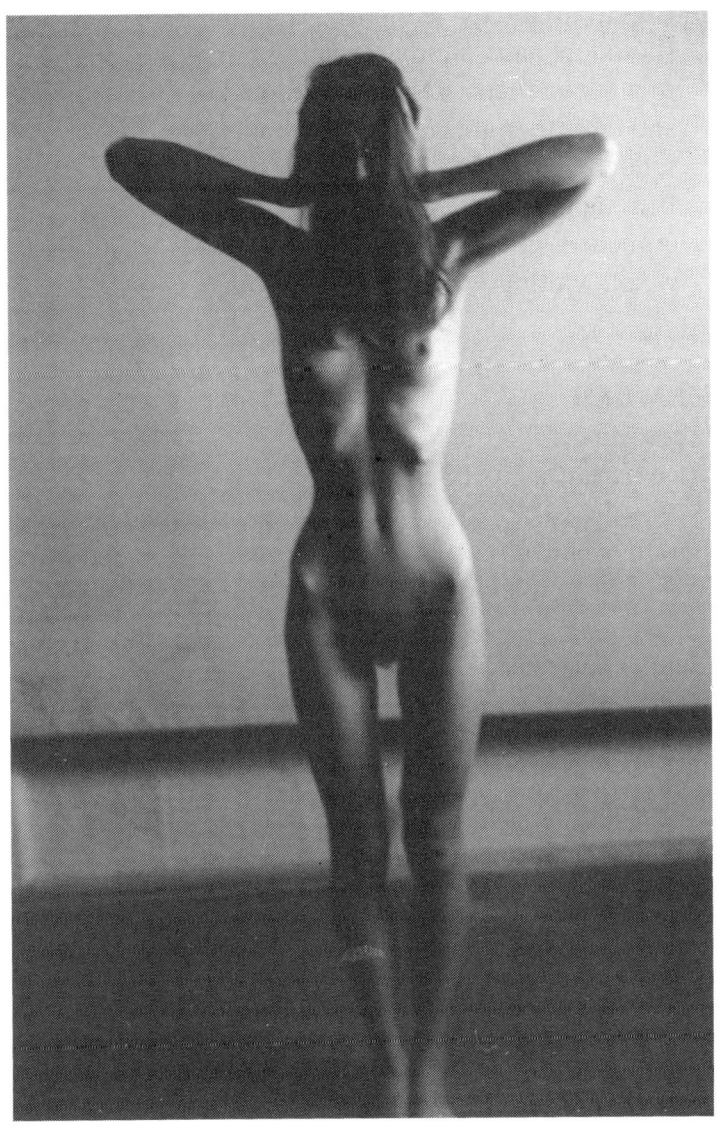

Photographed by Heidi Cable

When I'm happy and they stare I never care.
I walk tall ignoring it all.
But on tired days like these, standing here,
shoulders bare, shorts revealing limbs.
In a queue their eyes burn into me
and their thoughts,
sadden and anger.
I'm trapped at the check-out,
crouched on the floor,
weak, waiting, wishing.

SEPTEMBER
17th September 1994
There's a part of us that believes
                                        we can always be better
        more beautiful   so work out
                        work out that part first

20th September 1994
    21 today and sick on strong French fags.

21st September 1994 (5st 12lbs)

25th September 1994
MEAT TO LIVE
        NO   EAT TO LIVE BUT IT'S TOO LATE FOR
                    THE MEAT I HAVE EATEN.

INTERNAL TURMOIL
SELF INFLICTED
PERSONAL PAIN

29th September 1994
From today the following must happen. I will stop drinking alcohol; it is disrupting any normal eating habits by making me stuff myself stupid and also increasing sugar cravings. No more spoonfuls of that golden syrup etc PLEASE! I'm fed up of it going straight through me. Yes, then I won't feel so shitty (literally). Medical help/advice is now essential.

This happens when people hurt me, I become numb inside. Am I really so afraid of my emotions? Too powerful and painful for me to release. So now they are locked away, hidden from sight, deep inside, internalised.

30th September 1994
Thank God Emma came round this morning and got me up because feeling the way I did I would've spent the day in bed crying!

**I'M CLEANSING MY SOUL to ERADICATE
THE PAST and ERASE MEMORIES?**

OCTOBER
13th October 1994 (6st 5lbs)

31st October 1994 – Trebarwith Strand, Cornwall
Wandered along the cliffs. The urge to just run over the edge was, mmm, very strong. Pure temptation, almost too much. I feel ill, too much sugar in my system. I need help.

NOVEMBER
7th November 1994 (6st 6lbs) – *Felixstowe*
Injected with other people's memories in the arm and in the

hand.

DECEMBER
13th December 1994 (6st 1lb)
NEW YEAR – THE CUNNING PLAN!
- get a job
- be more outgoing
- start being more creative (something everyday)
- to stop spending my life in a blur!
- a new partner/new friends
- rebuild my super waif frame and watch that sugar and
  compulsive eating.
- eat and enjoy, not stuff.

Enveloped

Enveloped

1995

Enveloped

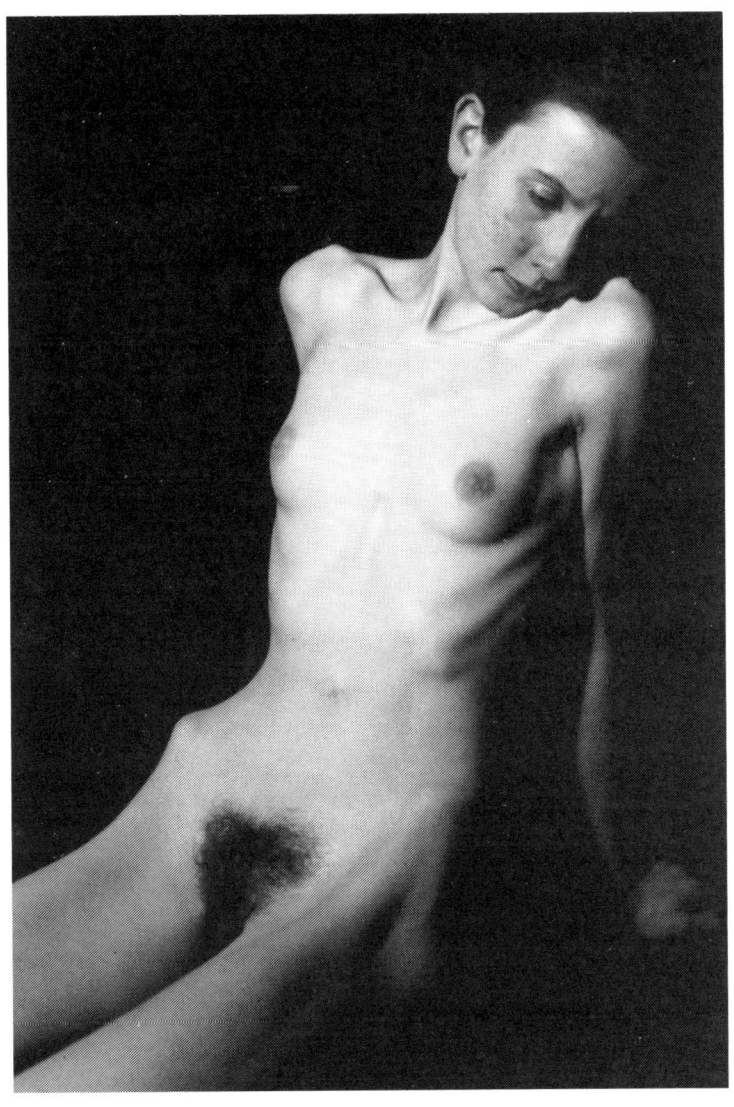

Photographed by Denis Taplin

Enveloped

JANUARY
5th January 1995
Hectic weather, wild wind, snow, a major chill. Good day though.

Have to say I've got chronic abdominal/stomach pain, it's been hanging around for a few days. Makes me lose interest in eating because I just feel full and bloated.

What have I saved at the end of the day? Impressions, memories, images of faces, places, sounds, colour.

8th January 1995
After stuffing myself I still feel so hollow and empty inside. For the first time I realise exactly what this feeling is, pure loneliness. I hate this. I really do need to find someone to share experiences with. I can't keep trying to fill the gap with food which I think is basically what I've been doing. Nurturing myself. It's time to face up to the fact I would love to have somebody there for me so I can feel, experience, love.

I know I have friends but it always seems to be me doing the ringing round and it makes me wonder if I wasn't prepared to keep my side of the contact whether they would even bother.

Enveloped

Am I really that . . .?

13th January 1995
Emotions:
Greatest joys are feeling happy, seeing friends.
Biggest fears are being inadequate, wasting my life. Sex.
Upset by a lonely, empty feeling.
Happy when I feel confident, unstoppable.
Angry when I feel an intense almost uncontrollable rage which
    scares me.
Crying caused by memories.
Nervous, I can't concentrate.
I feel good when I smile freely and glow.
I feel down when my whole being feels heavy.
For pleasure I read, especially comics, create and eat.
I admire my Mother, I love my Mum, Dad – who else?

FEBRUARY
1st February 1995
ME & MY SHADOW – WE TWO ARE ONE

7th February 1995
    People amaze me, thousands of us, all different, each
individual the creation of two others. And order and rules like
roundabouts. Everyday you do things perhaps not questioning
why. Are you really happy with your life? But there's so much
more. I've barely begun and feel I'll never look or truly feel as
an 'adult' should. There's nothing wrong with looking young.
Who is to say what 21 should be like, you only have those around
to compare with. Such a rush to act older than you really are, it
begins so young. No one seems happy to be their true age, striving
for adulthood through visual effects but maturity is something

46

that grows within, the mind expanding to accommodate experience and sometimes in that sense I feel truly informed. Yet I've only begun, there's still more. You have to create your own life and construct your own image. I've spent so long being serious, racing ahead for a better day, it's only now I'm beginning to realise . . .

10th February 1995
    Our arguments always leave me confused. I feel I should move out – you want me to be an adult, independent, WORKING. I know I will. I think you feel I'm wasting my time – sponging off the state. If I left home then that would be a form of independence, you wouldn't have to bother what I did. But then you say you love me and that it's not the money. I just shouldn't be letting myself down like this. WHICH WAY DO I TURN?

14th February 1995
    Offered a place at Derby.

20th February 1995 - Mural, St George's Hospital, Hornchurch
    The inevitable nightmare of . . . nothing is sorted at the hospital, lucky to get anywhere to sleep!
    Still, it's an experience so they say. Tried to go to London in the evening but it was hopeless, trains slow, delayed, so gave up and came back to Hornchurch.

21st February 1995
    Over halfway through the mural, pretty good going, eh! Evening went to Hornchurch and tried out The Cricketers (quiz night) and pretended to be French.
    'Pardon, je ne comprend pas!'
    'Right, we'll come back to you later!' What an attitude.
    Then to The Bull with its oh so welcoming barmaid Maria.

22nd February 1995
That corridor is freezing, so we're both pretty solemn and sombre, both just getting on with it. Finished by 5.30 p.m., bit of an anti climax. Sitting in silence in our room before going into Hornchurch.
Really wild, windy and cold.

23rd February 1995
On our way home. Saw De Kooning exhibition, being here reminds me of a scene from LA Story!

25th February 1995 (5st 13lbs)

27th February 1995
From within came five foetus at varying stages with limbs and beaded eyes. I gathered them up so pale, translucent and squeezed their soft rubber like forms. They began to squirm, retract, rapidly decaying and dissolving on a tray. A faint fishy air. I put them in a glass jar for keeps.

Tune into the feelings inside myself and trust them.
These are my first hand experiences.
They do not need to be validated by other people.

MARCH
6th March 1995 (5st 11lbs)
WON'T YOU PLEASE HELP ME – SOMEBODY
Just finished work and am now at the gallery. Feeling all . . . don't know whether it's tiredness . . .

16th March 1995
SACKED. Unsuitable for the position!

20th March 1995
Hospital 3 p.m. (at last), rectal examination.

23/24th March 1995
Body mass index 13.5. At 5st 12lbs I am only .5 away from brain dysfunction, 13 being the limit and 15 is still malnourished. Scary. It's a totally haunting thought. This explains why I feel completely off the planet, unable to concentrate, feeling dizzy, visual disturbances, tired, joint pains, headaches etc. I am literally so close to bodily shutdown, but at last some professional help and it's come just in time otherwise if I'd carried on struggling to gain weight by myself things could have reached a complete . . . I don't even want to consider it.

The dietician's a star, she is exactly what I need. I'm on a 6 meal a day plan which to begin with I thought, how on earth am I going to manage it, but even after today I feel so happy. I ate it all and can easily see myself eating more. It's wonderful, all the burden's been lifted off me. Help and support. I just have to give in and slow down. Lay down, relax, sleep when I feel like it. I am seriously ill right now.

Basically my system is so shot to buggery that it's bound to reject a lot of things; you just start to avoid certain foods, for me doughy, sweet foods because of the bingeing which would leave me freaked out and feeling extremely ill.

29th March 1995 (6st 0lbs)
GAINED 2lbs in a week! We're moving in the right direction although at the moment I'm feeling rank with back pain, stomach/ bowel area hurts. I've bloody well got thrush and my backside's buggering me about (you know what I mean).

So close to fading away, seriously this is life or death and I want to live.

APRIL

5th April 1995 (6st 2lbs)

I hate this immense feeling of tiredness. My body, especially my shins, ache constantly.

My concentration is shot to pieces. I forget.

11th April 1995

Indescribable feelings of physical pain, lethargy. It's all part of it. A theory suggested, we do these things for a reason. At the moment I don't understand why but in the end I'll be stronger for putting myself through this intensely eye opening phase.

No room for explanations, excuses.

12th April 1995 (6st 4lbs)

To be honest I just want to get it over and done with . . . I want my body back.

19th April 1995 (6st 4lbs)

I am feeling – ah – very let down by no one but myself.

Although at times I feel like screaming. I can't wait to eat when and what I want.

MAY

2nd May 1995

I'm sitting here wondering why I feel so, I guess, down. I lack lustre. Have to weigh myself tomorrow and see. The day when I can eat what I want and not have to be so preoccupied with food will be wonderful. Maybe this is what gets me down especially when I feel so rank.

Give me some good days soon.

I really do need more support than I'm receiving. I know it's a bit much to ask as people are probably fed up with the one

Enveloped

track topic. HOW DO YOU THINK I FEEL THEN?

I'M JUST SICK OF IT ALL.

3rd May 1995 (6st 6lbs)
We're getting back on course: INCREASE, INCREASE.
What a day, feeling tip top mentally and physically, like nothing can get me down. Plus it's beautiful weather, light and mmm sunny.

Thursday 4th May 1995
Afternoon . . .
Feeling pretty tired. It's stunningly lovely and sunny, so hot. I have to say though this is the first time for several weeks that my shins have started to ache again. You know, like somebody's kicked me. My stomach's blip blopping away so I'm obviously extremely hungry but instead of eating because I have to, indeed to succeed, thrive and survive, I'm also eating out of hunger. Practically every hour I'm eating something to boost my blood sugar levels and banish this odd feeling.
Evening . . .
I don't know who to turn to. I feel scared, extremely shaky now, leg pains intense, nauseous.
I hate feeling like this, having to just lay in bed, in silence. I want to be active and alive not bashing thoughts around my brain.

Friday 5th May 1995
Feeling very introverted, just need peace and quiet, unable to communicate properly or cope with noise. Although I have seen Emma and Jevan, both making a welcome break from my brain, I had to blow out, going to see a film this evening for purely selfish reasons.

51

Enveloped

What is wrong with me at the moment?
Why am I hurting so much?

ALL WE NEED TO MAKE OUR LIVES COMPLETE

Wednesday 10th May 1995 (6st 8lbs)
It's strange being able to feel this new flesh. I've been without
it for so long. There is no stopping me.

Sunday 14th May 1995
Freaky dream last night, it was all to do with my fish tank! I'd
bought two lizards to keep in it, someone took them away and
when I finally got them back they'd become huge and bug eyed
a bit like boa-constrictors, slithering, scary. Every time I
screamed at them they suddenly shrank and wriggled away. Then
they'd come back larger than before. Anyway it was horrible, I
tossed and turned all night.
It's getting near midnight. Can't sleep, my eyes feel sore and
tired. I'm very achy, generally. Also my insides feel as though
I'm being scraped out from within. It's horrible and painful,
maybe like a period cycle but without the blood, yet! Whatever,
it's doing me in. Also craving chocolate like I used to.
Ah ha, my new decisions are to stop being a life model . . .
which I've got to do as soon as possible because to be honest I
just don't want to show my body to others anymore. I don't
mind one to one but no more classes. Sign of a healthy new
attitude towards my developing body. I'm actually becoming in
tune with it, recognising and caring for myself. I have been and
think I still am scared by all this.
HOW COULD I DO THIS TO MYSELF?
Did I really not care about myself that much to want to
eradicate my existence. It's only now I'm reconnecting mind

and body. This time around I'm going to make damn sure I look after myself. When you've fucked up once, this seriously, there can be no turning back. EVER.

Monday 15th May 1995 (6st 7lbs)
Fuck! Need more food. Feel like an old dish rag, tired and washed out. Increase intake. At the moment there's not enough left at the end of the day to store.
I ache so much, extremely shaky and unbalanced. It scares me intensely.
I'm fascinated with circles, holes in things, negative spaces and shapes
If I stay in Felixstowe I will wither and fade,
this town is too small . . .

Friday 19th May 1995
It's alien nation day. The more I get stuck in a deadlock situation, the more they feed off the negativity and fuck me about, leaving me angry and confused. They create indecision and doubt.
What is wrong with me? (apart from the obvious!) And now it's raining again. I want the sun to brighten my mood and re-inject some enthusiasm into this body. Actually I'd feel a whole lot better if I didn't have diarrhoea but what can you do? FUCK YOU, because as a wise Matt Johnson said 'You can't destroy your problems by destroying yourself.'

Sunday 21st May 1995
Wow! What a weekend. Out on Friday evening with Emma and Jevan then last night I went to the Met! Ha ha. First time I've been out in Felixstowe on a Saturday night for, well, probably ever! Home at midnight (got a bit shaky and needed some food) but it was an interesting evening, didn't dance though

(felt the urge).

You know, seeing all those people I recognised made me realise (even though they may not know me and that's the way I prefer it to be in this town!) – yes it made me realise that if I stay here I'd just fade away. Inhibited: that's probably why I didn't get up and boogie. Not confident enough yet!

Luckily for me I have a goal: Derby here I come, and by then I will be fighting fit and through this shit. Somewhere I can start again, a clean slate with new people, new places.

Ha ha!

And today I haven't laughed so much for ages. Emma came round to help me slide my work, it took bloody ages to do – and that tripod! Aaaargh, who on earth invented those contraptions!!!

At the moment I'm just taking a break from a major clear out. Only a few select items are being salvaged from my past, out go old clothes etc, etc. Excess baggage. I prefer to be as minimal as is humanly possible. But we're moving soon, so farewell to this room that holds the memories of my withdrawal and restriction. It's good I no longer feel like I'm just trying to run away from life.

It's still Sunday evening and I've just made a startling realisation. You know I never realised how food obsessed I obviously used to be! So I've chucked out all my recipes and put my cookbooks downstairs. Jeez, and to think, this time last year I was working with the stuff practically everyday. Not good.

I just want and need a normal relationship with food instead of the chaos and disorder of the past.

Monday 22nd May 1995

All clear from the hospital, knew it would be, my internal me is my own stupid fault.

Enveloped

Tuesday 23rd May 1995

Boy, do I ache today! Leg muscles feeling really sore, taut, and my shins, oh, feel like someone's drained, is draining, the energy out of them. Useless limbs. Apart from that the sun is shining and it's warm. I'm dead chuffed with myself today, every opportunity I've taken and just gone with the flow instead of pondering. I've proudly said 'YES!' You know as I get better I begin to realise how odd I must have been to people, to my family especially. God knows how they managed to bear me. I feel like saying SORRY . . . not just a pathetic grovelling sorry but you made me realise.

I can't change the past but the future is mine.

Thursday 25th May 1995 (6st 8lbs)

I do remember saying in my early teens that if I wasn't careful I had the potential to become anorexic! And there was a stage when my Dad was badgering me about my eating. Also I once got a tad hysterical on the phone to Mum regarding the subject of my eating habits several years ago. I don't know, this seems to have been a long time coming, slowly building up over the years and now BANG! It's reached a life threatening crescendo.

I don't quite understand. All I ever wanted was some help which I didn't really get until things got to a serious crisis level. But maybe that had to happen first. This way I have and am still learning from experience. At least I'm making mistakes early in life so I can change things for the better, although this is a major cock up on a grand scale.

I will never treat myself so appallingly again, EVER and if I can help others I will because I know . . .

It's true about your environment reflecting you. I remember how I used to have loads of plants then I realised I'd just let them die, forgot to care for them, then I had none because I couldn't be bothered to look after them any more. So all my living creations withered away just as I was.

Right, here comes complete honesty. GUILT. I've only . . . I don't know, there have been times when I've started eating something then I guess a twinge of guilt kicks in and I've spat the food back out.

You see I'd only allow myself to taste it but not eat some of it properly, and the pondering, 'Should I, shouldn't I.' Aliens! but then I don't understand why because I have wanted to regain my weight for a long while so they were obviously lurking in the depths but never got a secure hold: subconsciously I've been trying to fight them. Only now am I realising that they did, do exist.

Tuesday 30th May 1995

How can this be happening. 'She's gone, Amy.' Emily, if there's a chance you're alive . . . I'm wishing for a miracle. News at midnight, one woman dead, another woman and man missing, swept away.

Numb and lost. Em, I keep expecting you to bounce back but this time . . .

JUNE

4th June 1995

It's now Sunday. I've never had to cope with anything like this before. I'm very screwed up. Em loved life. I smile when I think of her, she's a beautiful person. She'd want you to get up there and at 'em and not be sad. Spent most of the week in and out of bed deeply grieving.

Sunday 18th June 1995 (6st 9lbs)

Yesterday was good, decided to go rollerskating! Haven't done it since I was 8 or 9. The place was full of kids and there's me plodding along, determined not to fall over which I managed not to!

Then in the evening out with Poo and Clare, spent it in the pub drinking and playing shithead, then to the club where fucking nosey two faced bitch came over and started to go on about Emily to Emma which completely unnerved her, she was really upset. God that girl, if she hadn't have gone off I was going to tell her to just 'FUCK OFF.' Emma said she felt like decking her, that would have been just excellent. So we came back to mine and just chatted until 2 a.m. about how we felt, about Em.

You can't share it with anyone who didn't know her.

Been thinking about Em a lot. I'm really missing her. Feeling physically pretty crap (kidney/urinary infection, so am on antibiotics). On the brink of tears, don't know what to do with myself, nervy, restless, scared. So I'm sitting on the beach crying. I don't want them to find her body, not now. This is how it should be, she's gone.

Monday 26th June 1995
THEY'VE FOUND HER BODY. I WISH THEY HADN'T.

Friday 30th June 1995
Feeling mental today, not entirely happy but it's gorgeously sunny. Think I'm just tired. Not sleeping well, nightmares. When I woke last night, felt like screaming, scared. Been smoking all week.

Let me rest in peace for a while.

JULY
Monday 3rd July 1995
There's only one way to describe how I'm feeling, DEPRESSED. Yesterday I considered running off, but where?

That wouldn't solve anything. You can change your surroundings but no matter how far you run you can't hide from yourself. A lot of this is due to tiredness, it's almost like I won't let myself sleep. I woke drenched in sweat and crying at 3 a.m. I went to bed at 9 but couldn't rest. Last time I looked at the time it was 1.39 a.m. and I had to leave the light on. Maybe I'm just neurotic!

Need to relax, calm down and rest because I'm mentally draining myself at the moment.

Get a grip and get a life, Amy, for everyone's sake.

Wednesday 19th July 1995

Foggy-headed today, lacking lustre and motivation. I'm just looking forward to leading a normal life, fulfilling, instead of this non-whatever-it-is crap. Why do I keep suffering from vaginal itching and infection when swabs return as normal? Doughy food, bloating, a lot of sugary things, make it worse.

AUGUST

Sunday 20th August 1995

I wish I could smash my fist through the window, watch it shatter but feel no pain.

Life can be so full of sadness. One minute everything seems fine then you're stumbling along the beach with tears in your eyes. I'm thinking of Em and the birthday present I can no longer give to her: I bought it months before. But Rothko remains.

Enveloped

Enveloped

1996

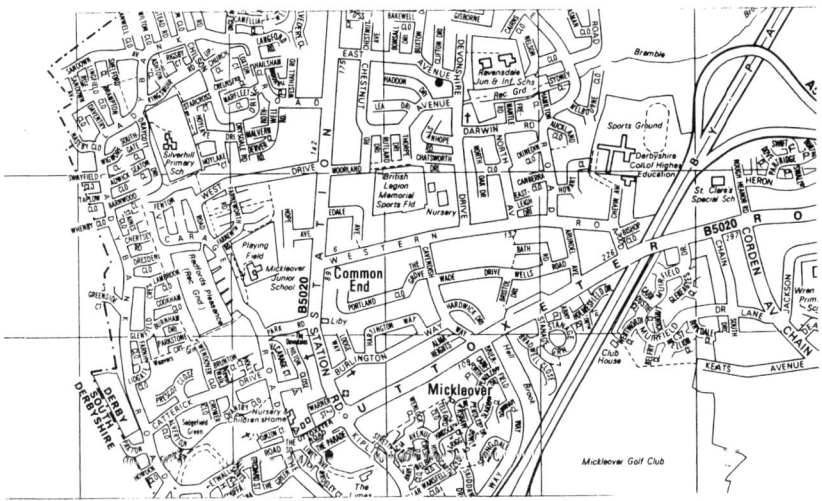

JANUARY

6th January 1996 - Derby

Today is the first time I have felt really sexually frustrated. It's true, if I had the chance right now I'd love to. I'm just all restless and tingly. You know, I'm better, getting stronger each day and I've got my body back. I keep looking down and there are my breasts! I touch and feel them and yes, they're real. SEX in '96. It's all coming back to me. Sure I'm scared, it's been so long but it's got to be done.

MARCH

14th March 1996

From tomorrow, I – Amy Phillips, do solemnly swear to stop binge eating. Help. So until I am capable of concentrating on proper foods instead of constantly snacking (which is getting ridiculous and out of control) I must refrain from buying bags of sweets, chocolate bars, chocolate products, orangeade and crisps. I hate myself for doing this so why is it happening again? I want to hide.

Enveloped

15th March 1996

Today I've been to see a counsellor. It's true. I'm on the brink of losing my grip on reality. After bingeing last night I feel really rank! In an attempt to make me feel – it worked, but it's pain.

When I stop talking I look scared, my eyes give me away. Essentially I feel scared. It's a constant battle between my two sides, the part that is all for giving in to madness and the other that knows I'm capable of great things. I need to express myself and this pent up frustration and anger; to feel would be so good because I'm purely a shell.

'What do your questions tell you about my psychological state?' He can see I've been hurt very badly and am still hurting. Conscious eye contact with him. I'm looking for answers or direction to the root of it all, because I don't know who I am . . .

16th March 1996

Things are OK. Had to get out and get away so I went into town. Oh yeah, I've hidden by dying my hair black which is cool. I feel a bit more solid. Spontaneous purchases! Dangly earrings, tartan trousers, jeans, skirt etc. I'm so pleased, oh and a lacy black bra. More feminine clothes. It's to boost my self esteem. The bra is essential!

Today I seem to be able to face people. 'Trainspotting' with Dan. Came back and drank almost demonically. So much for no sweets and chocolate. I've fucked that up already. Then there's Tim, intense conversation. Why do I need to know where I stand? Because I know but . . . I just don't know how or what to feel. I'd just love to be loved. Perhaps I need some sex. I won't allow myself to feel in case it's something I want but know I can't have, it's out of reach. I'm scared of getting hurt and losing out to ugly fat girls.

What is wrong with me? Am I really that grim?

In fact the conclusion is that I have an immense urge to destroy

myself. I don't want to kill myself – just destroy with . . . chemicals, alcohol, scabs, self attack. I've got to stop drinking but it calms the aggression.
Lust for life?

Feeling isn't weakness
Feeling isn't weakness

Feeling isn't weakness . . .

running away from yourself is.

17th March 1996
I NEED TO GET MYSELF STRAIGHT

18th March 1996
Nightmare, walking along a very high concrete ridge with Tanya. Waves on one side, looking out over the sea. I threw a mug into the sea, it bounced back and chipped a chunk out of the concrete. No colour. Waves growing bigger, I carried on walking, anxious, they're getting larger, lapping over edge of ridge. Water burning my bare feet. Trying to get away before it engulfs me, climbing over the side, water still following me. Stepping. Look back. Enormous wave bearing down on me. Foot touching down on soil. Wake up scared and freaked out.

19th March 1996
Tim cried . . . by destroying myself I'm hurting him because I'm going to a place he can't get to and he's not strong enough to bring me back at the moment. Thinks I don't love him any more, how wrong he is. I just don't feel. I know I'm obviously immensely fucked up at the moment but don't feel it, don't feel anything only physical pain from the bingeing. He's scared, I'm scared. The only one who can stop all this is me so now I'm on cold turkey. Binge food confiscated. So tonight is the first night

in the fight for freedom. I've still eaten more than is comfortable but HAVE NOT binged so it's a start. Instead I've made a start on a piece of art, expressing repressed emotions, physicality, aggression, anger. It all needs a release, sexually?

Tim fears loss of my life and love but I think I'm going to lose him.

22nd March 1996

I know I must go back and see Mum and Charlie at Easter. At Christmas I said I wouldn't but I just have this feeling . . .

What do I do now?

I no longer want others to treat me as though I'm fucked in the head.

I don't want to go back to Mum's. I have left.

I do want to be here in Derby but am not concerned about getting a degree, it's the way of life I need.

23rd March 1996

Live for now, you only get one shot at this life. Buy what you want, need who you need, desire what you've denied.

24th March 1996

Maybe I've found my direction or at least an enthusiasm for writing. It's my little fantasy at the moment to work for a paper. I mean, I love reading, writing. I can do this if I just put my mind to it.

Evening . . . God I'm doing it again, this seriously over-eating getting dangerously close to binge. Threw some biscuits away because I knew I was going to finish them all if I didn't lose them somewhere. Why am I doing this? Feeling rank, uncomfortable, hot, can't sleep. Wish Tim was awake, need distracting. WHY, WHY, WHY? Definitely feeling a tad on the sexual side. Earlier I had a really bad urge to kiss Tim passionately but I didn't. It's not the done thing is it? Misdirected desire? Is sexual frustration behind all this? Obviously!

Questions, questions, when will the answers become clear, clear enough for me to act. Shit, am I ever going to get straight? 'Hang in there, P,' as Tim would say. I'm trying but . . .

26th March 1996

You know essentially I'm sorted, it is purely boredom that destroys me. The fact things are mundane, easy. As Tim says it's more exciting to be fucked up. I still need to control my eating better. My problem time is the evening. I have work to do but can't get motivated so I sit and eat, purely for comfort. I need more in my life.

Sharing with Tim next year, I'm scared of committing myself to something I want but know will hurt me. We, Tim and I . . . well it's not strange but if you think about it, it is, our friendship, the physicality, but it's lovely and makes me feel alive.

28th March 1996

I ache so badly today. I hate feeling like shite, it just does my head in!

29th March 1996

I've been thinking about how I was this time last year and it's a damn scary thought. My journals show it all happening.

30th March 1996

I love writing! I came to bed and couldn't get settled, just kept thinking about what else I could eat but instead managed to resist and after picking my face a little I decided to carry on with my story. In a way it's describing my state of mind at times but it's also a grimmer side of I guess having an eating disorder. I didn't intentionally set out this way, it's how it's developed.

31st March 1996

Topic of sexuality. I think, well I know, I'm scared of sex. I want to do it, I can see myself do it but you know, when it comes to the crunch, it makes me fucking cringe. I'm used to protecting myself, and penetration, sex, is forcing me to feel, and as much as I want it, I'm frightened of what will happen.

APRIL

1st April 1996

I DON'T KNOW WHAT TO DO WITH MY ANGER AND HURT

2nd April 1996

I can't believe how happy I felt yesterday. Spent the day constructively in lectures and studying, then got blasted in the evening. Sitting on the balcony with Tim was just heaven. If only life was always like that. Still feel a little tipsy this morning! I have got to get some decent sleep!!! It's 8.30 p.m. and I'm stuffed with an aching gut. Just hyper tonight, have gobbled several bars of chocolate. Why?

I'm orally fixated this evening. It fucking hurts.

Tim's gone. I feel like crying. I think I'm going to start my periods again soon. Keep getting loads of transparent, elastic discharge especially in the morning. Been feeling bloated as well for a couple of days. God I hate myself. I'm such a fucking mess.

3rd April 1996

2 a.m. . . . . masturbated for the first time in 3 years and it felt good.

4th April 1996
Feeling very calm and relaxed. I love sitting in the sun.

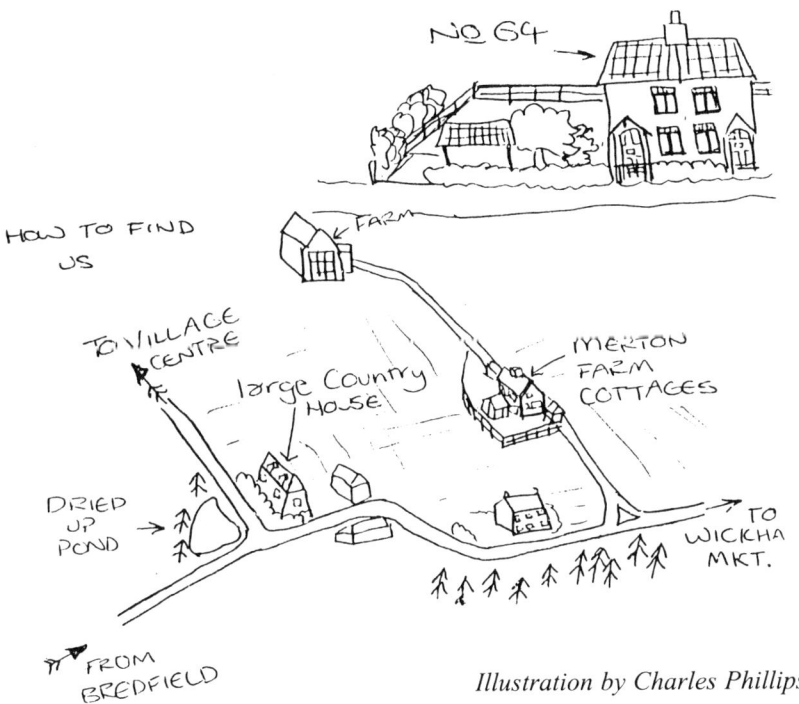

NO 64 →

HOW TO FIND
US

TO VILLAGE
CENTRE

FARM

large Country
HOUSE

MERTON
FARM
COTTAGES

DRIED
UP
POND →

TO
WICKHA
MKT.

FROM
BREDFIELD

Illustration by Charles Phillips

6th April 1996 – Dallinghoo
PERIODS RESTARTED

Yes it's true! I can't quite believe it but I have the proof. It's 3 years since they stopped, roughly a year since I decided to live and about 6 months that I've been maintaining a decent weight.

Before I came back I thought I must take some tampons!!!

I WASN'T GOING MAD, JUST WAITING . . .

Well, I'm getting there now, it's just accepting who and what I am and being content with the way life is. At the moment I do feel truly content. I like myself as well. The periods explain why I've felt fucking bloated and big round the sides and eating so much. I obviously needed it, especially the chocolate! God, I'm a woman again.

7th April 1996
Quite content and happy in myself.

9th April 1996
Been in one of those eating moods. I'll make the effort not to pick so much tomorrow, well it's something to do isn't it!!!

10th April 1996
I NEED TO PROTECT MYSELF. Aaaargh! I did it again. Stupid girl.

15th April 1996
Feeling turned on again. I'm getting seriously frustrated. I ache like hell internally, my back and limbs. Tired, restless, can't seem to sleep.

16th April 1996
For fuck's sake, Amy, get a grip! I've eaten shit loads, binge style over the last hour. Feeling bloated and ill. WHY, WHY, WHY? because I'm restless, bored but now I feel fat – not fat exactly but uncomfortably wide. I think when I feel uncomfortable I panic and eat more to induce more pain.
Too much going in and nothing coming out!
START AGAIN TOMORROW.
MODERATE EATING AND MINIMAL SNACKING.
It's when I eat proper meals, it all goes to shit. I still want more . . . to fill the hole.

20th April 1996 – Derby
3 days of being good.

21st April 1996

Strange dream last night where I'd gone to see Dad and ended up going for Granny Phillips, swearing at her, pushing her and eventually smashing her head into a mirror! Weird shit.

23rd April 1996

This is just so strange, I've been on the phone for nearly an hour discussing possibilities. I can't believe he called after that letter. God, what is going on? Whatever happens I'm going for it. I'm not sure if it's the right thing to do but . . .

30th April 1996

I am just so tired, my shins are fucking painful, my head is full of garbage and hurts. I always feel fucking tired. I don't even do anything to get this way. So why?

MAY

1st May 1996

I am not happy today, fucking aching, tired, headache and the beat goes on. Fucking irritable as well. The girls' giggling is winding me up something chronic. I can't find any peaceful space today.

13th May 1996

Today I am immensely angry. Just seething away and the whole world can just shove themselves up their own arse. I don't need any fucker, they only let you down whether they intend to or not. Need to get my stability and self ease back because at the moment I feel intensely restless, agitated, uneasy, want to run away but I'll never manage to lose myself.

14th May 1996
Feeling quite mischievous today and content. I just ache intensely, limbs, stomach, lower back.

15th May 1996
Why is it always up to moi to sort things out? I end up giving myself fucking therapy and yes I am slightly annoyed with it all.

22nd May 1996
Feeling frustrated and bored, tired and bloated, uncomfortable with myself.

26th May 1996
Dreamt of sharks last night. Everything's in slow motion, heavy.

30th May 1996 – Felixstowe
After 3 years I've done it, conquered the fear.

JUNE
4th June 1996 – Derby
I'm so tired at the moment. Fuck knows why. It's like my limbs are being drained and my brain wanders off onto another plain. I am in pain.

I'm back in Derby. It has to be said I've felt so relaxed and happy in Felixstowe, after all this time and everything that's happened. Who would have thought it?

6th June 1996
Am I hiding being here? Hell, who knows, maybe the summer will make life clearer.

Enveloped

13th June 1996 – Cornwall

14th June 1996
Depression is hanging over me, I just can't shake it off. DAY 2. I'm in Cornwall

22nd June 1996 – Felixstowe
I've been meaning to write in this for days. Why do I suffer from depression so badly? You know my self esteem has been practically non existent these past days. I just can't function. I'm left feeling worthless. I don't know why I can't live for myself apart from the fact that I have no image of a self. Trying to be positive, I do have these moments. Looking for some work to fill the empty hours until I can go back and hide in Derby.

There's got to be a reason why I'm alive or even still alive. I have no desire to kill myself but I'm left thinking, what is the point? Life is pointless, or maybe it's just mine.

WORTHLESS
POINTLESS
STRUGGLE
SCARED

JULY
2nd July 1996
Feel bloated, tearful, stressed. Just keep crying, can't get comfortable, agitated. I hate getting this low, everything feels out of control, I wanna disappear.

6th July 1996
The only eventful thing was me cutting my finger (very crappily) then just completely losing it and blacking out cold in

the shop. It was really scary. I said, I think I'm gonna be sick. I could taste blood in my mouth, got very hot and cold then my vision disintegrated and bam – I fell to the floor! Nice one. I thought I was tucked up in bed dreaming when I finally came round. It's like you hear what's happening around you but can't respond.

Anyway I've slept for 3 hours out of the past 48. Well hyper, but also very shaky and sick inside from lack of it. I'm fed up of being on my own.

7th July 1996

My last thought before sleep was about giving myself a black eye . . .

8th July 1996

Being here has opened old wounds, ones I fear will never heal. I'm living in shadows. Being here is hard, harder because I am the past. What was it, 'self obsessed, self absorbed.' Hell I thought I'd come further but no. Maybe I am. I'm certainly mentally screwed up bigtime. I should never have got back into this . . . never come here.

I hate what I am. Fed up of eating and existing. Sometimes I feel I'm going to scream violently if I force myself to have another mouthful.

WHAT EVER HAPPENED TO HAPPINESS?

13th July 1996

I'm now on Lustral (lust for life) so let's hope it helps, and also penicillin because my throat's inflamed. Things are OK, just feeling shite and tired, shaky etc, etc. Need to get a decent night's sleep.

Enveloped

17th July 1996
I FEEL BEATEN . . .

24th July 1996
I dreamt about Richey again last night. I bumped into him on a train platform, we were both working in the café. I saw him sweeping the platform and went out to him. Where the tracks were it was full of deep water like a canal. I spoke to him and we hugged, just stood still in each other's arms. He looked quite drawn. I remember it felt like hugging my brother because he was so thin. Very real sensations.

I live more in my dreams than I do in life.

I MUST LUST RAL

My head is left mid space
This lustral to give me
Lust for life
Has left me dead.
Feel no sorrow
Feel no pain
No desire . . .

All this banished to quell
the longings,
The need to express,
Experiment and fulfil
To quench the frustrations
That drain
And hold me in torment.
When all distractions are gone
And once again
I am alone.

75

AUGUST

3rd August 1996

I'm feeling really down today, in despair. I sat on the prom and thought about jumping off the pier so I had to walk away before I did it. I don't want to die, I just want to be happy.

6th August 1996

No more Lustral for me. Need a little more spark than sleep so it's time to make the break and see what happens.

8th August 1996

There's stuff I can't reconcile. When I'm back in Derby it'll be easier, it won't be in my face. I'll have my own life and loves back. I miss Tim so much. I've been thinking about asking him out but I don't know, it's all so confusing.

Nightmares surrounding sleep. Agitated, uneasy.

14th August 1996

Need to eat properly and stop this continuous snacking and overeating. Less snacks, more real, wholesome stuff. ESSENTIAL FOR MENTAL WELL BEING because I hate myself when I eat too much especially when it's all sweet, sugary shite. Uggh! I feel so sick.

23rd August 1996

Dreams of fishes which started on Felixstowe beach. I'd swum out too far and could see the tower in the distance. My feet kept feeling things in the water and I was trying to keep myself afloat but getting scared, panicking, and the water was grim and murky. Then the next thing I know I'm reclining in a boat, naked, basking in the sun and fish were leaping out of the water and into the boat, so I put them back into the sea and they carried on. There was one really impressive fish, all eel like with a massive spine and transparent skin. The water was clear so I could see it snaking along. It spoke to me.

Next thing I'm being washed up on the beach and all I can hear is the shingle being dragged by the waves. Then I'm sitting huddled with a towel around me on a steep bank of pebbles. People were around me, talking, but I was completely isolated, quiet and numb. Couldn't move or speak, just watching.

Then still in the towel, I got out of Mum's Volvo at Nunnery Court. We walk my bags to a door but never make it there. Images of the building, music, noise. It's late, Charlie is also there and I keep jumping over the little fences. I'm dressed in black leggings and blue t-shirt, my legs are very thin.

24th August 1996

Nightmares, nightmares so bad I woke up screaming and bawled my eyes out. Maximum of 4 hours sleep per night at the moment. Toothache, aspirins and alcohol. Tormenting myself with hatred, bitterness and anger at being treated like shit. Paranoia setting in.

SEPTEMBER

1st September 1996

Sometimes just being, staying alive, is exhausting.

6th September 1996

Emotionally strange day. I felt very calm, mentally on a plane, clear and free, then driving back from Mum's for no identifiable reason I was overwhelmed by I don't know . . . I just started crying, there was rage, bitterness, sadness inside there for a while. Very odd.

17th September 1996 – Derby

Update time . . . now in Derby, at home and happy. Still no T yet.

Things are sorted but I've never seen him look so unhappy as he did, as he does. It's been a bizarre triangle of a summer with emotional games but I'm home and it's out of my face. It's time to move forward and live for now, not what was or could've been or still could be but these passing moments and people are what matters. I'm crashing, the tiredness is catching up on me and I ache like a bastard.

22nd September 1996

Feeling homesick which is a bit of a contradiction because WHERE IS MY HOME? WHAT IS HOME? But I just miss Mum, wish I could see her today.

23rd September 1996

Don't know if it's true . . . T won't be coming back. I do love T incredibly and no matter where he is that will never change. It's the one thing I know, if nothing else.

24th September 1996

Feeling very pissed at the moment and it's not even 9 o'clock. Feel like ringing someone. God my head is, ugh, off in space. Too much cold cure and alcohol, a bad combination!!! Got stressed about workload.

26th September 1996

FUCK FUCK FUCK

Black. The colour of the dead.

30th September 1996

Monday nights are a fucking nightmare. Walked out, too much

pain and pressure.

OCTOBER
7th October 1996
Feeling very down today and washed out, it's the atmosphere.

14th October 1996
5 months and still no period.

14th October 1996
Feel like I've been beaten up today, aching and in much pain.
Went and saw Charlie yesterday, he's looking in great shape.

16th October 1996
Feeling utterly depressed and trapped.

The mirror reflects back at me
a sight I do not want to see,
panda eyes and bruised lips.
Ugliness
This self hatred colours all perception.
I'm left seeing lies, illusions
created inside to make me hide
when I'm not strong enough to fight.

Sometimes it's hard to see
when your eyes are the size of peas.

31st October 1996
Over the past few days I've been coming out of my depression;
the past week of nightmares is over. Feeling good but like I'm
going into overdrive.

NOVEMBER
16th November 1996

4 p.m. my head went completely funny. I'd felt very shaky this morning and then levelled out but this afternoon my vision started vibrating; felt so weak and shaky I thought I was going to collapse. Feverish, intense sensitivity to noise, head hurting like someone was screwing blinkers into my skull, became scared and trapped and I could feel plummeting depression approaching which I'm trying to keep at bay.

19th November 1996

It's snowing. Walked to Tesco's and back in the blizzard, it was lovely in a snowy sort of way, the rest of the time I've been working. Quite impressive.

22nd November 1996

Well, I'm still in no man's land, feeling calm but have started being really tired.

Wednesday I did another self portrait looking a lot happier.

Thursday was a limbs-like-lead day, got up for breakfast then collapsed back into bed for a few hours.

Friday, headachy, tired, achy limbs but still OK.

26th November 1996

Ian has been here this weekend and it's been lovely. Very calm almost to the point of non-existence. But what do you do when you can't live with someone and can't live without them?

28th November 1996

I've been thinking, I'm still calm, but I'm wondering how fine the line is between calmness and depression. It's hard to tell the difference. Today has been OK though, had a lay in and got on with my work and that's it really.

DECEMBER
5th December 1996

Since I've moved out of the house into room 418 I am so much happier, I keep smiling. All the pressure on my head has been lifted. I'm self contained, feeling empowered and enjoying the fact I don't know anyone here: no need to talk to people. It's a good time to be by myself, just to be. I'm going to stick at University because if I do then T should return and it's one way we can be together.

I've been thinking, I'm very sensitive to atmospheres and when I'm with other people I lose my sense of self and almost independence which is very odd. I lose what's me and not me.

I am feeling more me.

13th December 1996 (7st 5lbs)

81

1997

JANUARY
1st January 1997 – Felixstowe
I've spoken to T twice today.
Well, resolutions are made to be broken, but I've decided over the coming months I shall manage my depression and mania more successfully so that it doesn't rule my days so much. Be positive and embrace what each day brings with minimal dread. Find my creative self again and express . . .

9th January 1997
Saw Mum earlier and I finally cried, it helped reduce the tension in my neck. I'm so down at the moment, it's like I'm giving in, everything seems futile, pointless. My entire life lacks meaning and direction. Mum really touched me, she said whatever I do doesn't matter as long as I'm happy. Then speaking to T, he doesn't know what to do but we kind of talked about him coming back to Derby, I leave University, get a job and live together, it might be the only way to kick-start this life. If I remain here, I'll be in suspended animation for the next one and a half years when all I want to do is live.

11th January 1997
I think I regress into silence. I was thinking about the group and how I rarely speak, my silence is my resistance and also regression. It's not a sulking like I did when I was younger, more a withdrawal, not wanting to communicate. The biggest problem is that I hate people; being alone is an easier option but possibly not the right thing because I'm aware I'm withdrawing. In a way I want to go back to Derby to be alone because there I can go all day without seeing or speaking to anyone.
I don't know why other people annoy me, maybe it's their stupidity and the effort it takes to engage in banality with them. Of course I genuinely do like and love some people, but very

few.

12th January 1997 – Derby

Spoke to T and he's not coming back to Derby at all so a new dilemma is underway. He really wants me to go and visit him and spend some quality time, just us. So the possible options are that I can leave University and go live and work in Keswick which would suit me, but first I need to suss it out, OR stay at University but go spend the summer in Keswick, which seems like a gentler solution so that way I don't give everything up. Oh man.

I'm just drawn to T and he means so much to me that things need to be done for the right reason.

OH BOLLOCKS!

16th January 1997

Feeling good about myself, even quite sexy!

17th January 1997 (Eight and a half months and no blood)

Huh (big sigh). Feeling in deep fucking despair today, don't know why, directionless and very tired. I had made some positive decisions this week to get up and live which involves me learning, changing and acknowledging my existence and my body, to look after it and find confidence in it. Basically, to make the most of what I have, rather than to live in regret. I'm going to start swimming and yoga again. I need to feel beautiful inside and love who I am, enough to take the time to care for myself. I just don't know what to do with my life. Looking at the work to do for this term I really can't be bothered. Aaargh. Too depressed to eat properly. No, no, no. Tim's here too. I had a bizarre dream about him and was convinced I'd wake up and be in Keswick. I thought maybe I'd dreamt T was here but he is and . . .

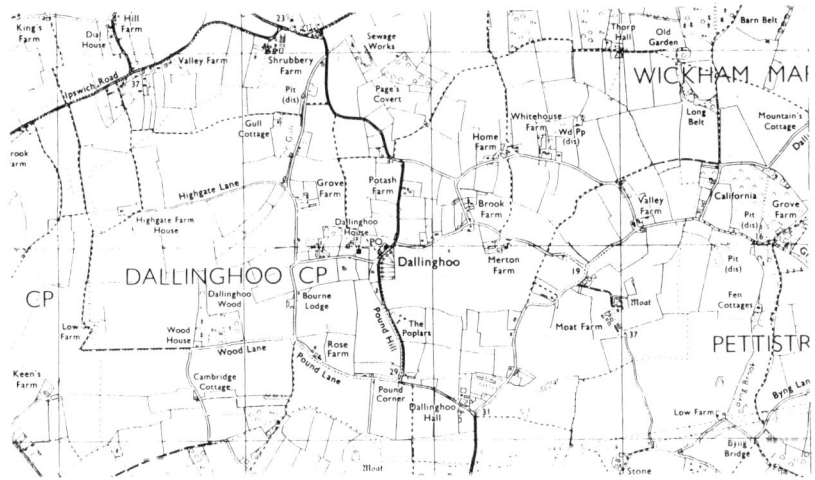

25th January 1997 – Dallinghoo

Well here we are, it's now Saturday and I'm back living at Mum's. I've left University and it's been a mad week. Basically seeing T went to shit. He came to say goodbye last Saturday morning and he looked so ill, he scared me, he really scared me and it was deeply distressing and upsetting. Nothing was resolved and it made me realise I'm not strong enough for both of us. I can barely keep myself from buckling as it is. Spoke to Mum and just ended up crying about how unhappy and down I was and she said there was always a place for me with her if I wanted to leave.

So finally, after much crying, frustration, anger, I decided on Monday morning to set it all in motion and make the break. Since doing it, well, it feels right, I mean, there's a whole new load of stuff to face and resolve but I can't survive in a rut anymore.

Wednesday I came back. I'm not scared any more but I do realise how insecure I'd become, never knowing where I could return to and instead clinging to my room unable to face people. You know how you can sense a crisis looming, well that was

87

how it felt. I mean I may have flown but it's better than retreating further into the unsocial, suspended and solitary world, or rather the side of my mind that is fearful of everything. Now I have to get on and get a life of some description.

26th January 1997
Felt pretty shitty, anxious, restless, been walking. It's frustration really, at least I'm eating proper meals now even though I don't feel hungry. If I was still on my own I'd probably be living on thin air.

1997 is going to be a year of great change. This year I need to make headway so I stop getting ill. Then all I'd like is for my life to get a little easier.

FEBRUARY
1st February 1997
Feeling very over tired, sick, ill, fragile, weak and want to give in, just collapse. Feverish. Not been sleeping particularly well these past few days.
HOLLOW EYES
HOLLOW HEAD
Been OK earlier, had some chocolate and it made me feel rank; actually I think I had that crème egg on Tuesday which tasted odd and since then . . .

Steer clear of chocolate for a little while, also might be an idea to reduce to a minimum the amount of sweets I'm getting through; all that unnecessary sugar could be what's draining. So I'll try as of tomorrow. It helped last time.

Really I'm sick of fighting the looming disintegration. WHY CAN'T I JUST BREAK DOWN (please Amy, please . . .)

Enveloped

Rain splatters on the pane
It sounds so loud it hurts my brain
and the system's pumping hot and cold
I hear it bubble, hiss and clank
the metal piping near the tank.

Draughts they whistle round my head
So I curl up tight beneath the bed
But still they find me clutching bone
as I rest upon the telephone.

And the TV's talking to itself
as I wonder if you've ever felt
The urge to melt into the floor
and leave a stain,
forever more.

2nd February 1997
    Feeling shit and tearful interspersed with moments of strength.

3rd February 1997
    Survived day one of work although in the afternoon I went so
cold that I wanted to come home! Nicely tired.

12th February 1997
    Don't know why, feeling desperately down today. I've got a
dodgy tum and a squidgy bum and what feels like the beginnings
of thrush. FAB! Possible culprits I know, but I just indulged.
Urrrgh . . .

17th February 1997
    When I think about the future I just want to cry.

A day in Dallinghoo drifts by,
just the dog and I.
We potter and pace around the house,
remaining silent,
voicing doubts,
about the way life should be led
and sometimes I just wish for bed
but unlike our dog I can't justify
these movements circular and uninspired.

Been dreaming about dead horses which were being kept in stables even though they'd rotted to bone and some were just suspended ribcage. I remember saying, you keep these because you're unable to accept they're dead, and a large white rat which our dog tried to swallow, and the following evening it was found whole inside a dead woman.

26th February 1997
It's 3.19 p.m. and at this very moment I feel peace, even a happiness radiating inside. The past week has been full of depression, discontent and disheartenment. I have got to make sure I start eating more food to compensate for my weight loss. It's not deliberate, it's just that when I'm like this I'm not inspired to eat, though I still do, but you lose the hunger, lose the interest and it all tastes the same. Uninspiring. But I will not let it happen again. I can't allow entrapment into anorexia. There is too much at risk and to risk second time around.

MARCH
11th March 1997
Well, what hasn't happened since I last wrote in here! Been to see Mary because it's all going to shit in the weight department.

I look fucking appalling, ribs are sticking through, breasts disappearing etc, etc. Basically I've relapsed. Anorexia is back but it's different this time, more subtle; whereas before it was a highly motivational force and controlled all areas of my life and behaviour. Now it's crept back through, and it takes advantage of my don't care, disinterested attitude to most things. Like I say you offer me a gourmet meal or a piece of toast and I'd go for the toast and you see that's how it's working away, cunning.

It's like there's me, and beside me sits my anorexia; it has more identity than I do. It keeps reaching into me trying to reattach itself and I'm aware I have to stop this because once you fall below a certain weight threshold the brain turns itself off; you're no longer capable of rational thought and that's when the anorexia has won and got control of the whole person as routines set in. I have to fight back. Whatever I am I deserve better than this. I'll not be dragged back through the shittiness again.

It's still so near. If I can get away from it this time then . . . I don't want to spend the rest of my life stuck in stupid cycles of recovery and relapse. If I want to die I should just finish it once and for all instead of slowly and continuously destroying this body and brain. The problem is I can't let myself – I don't want to die but I don't want to live like this, in a no man's land, directionless, scared, frustrated, sad, alone, not knowing who I am, who I can be. My depression gets so fucking bad, I get so fucking desperate and I hear the negative voices and thoughts racing. Lithium has been suggested but . . . that's pretty heavy shit.

Easter is fast approaching so I'll see T. Then I decide, another crossroads. KESWICK – to move or not to move? I'm inclined to do it anyway, there is nothing to lose. If T can sort things out and is seriously up for it then to live together would be . . . it might help both of us. I love him and there is so much unexpressed and stuff to share. I want the chance to feel again and stop being so self contained. I want a fucking life.

22nd March 1997

It's been shit all the way, anxiety management and I end up at St Clements distraught and on edge. They don't take me seriously enough. I still have no means of managing my depression. They doubt its severity. The only way of convincing is by taking drastic action but it would be futile.

Eating is very sporadic, from sticking to the plan then picking at bits. Aaaargh.

23rd March 1997

Today I feel sick and pale (eating good amount though), my feet are so sore, itchy, inflamed that I would love to just pull and cut the callouses right out. I can't believe how painful they are, I've even bandaged them up. I want to rip and tear at the skin.

I'm 23 and my body is fucked. The ibuleve is giving me indigestion something cruel. I could just neck a bottle of red. You can't concentrate when your feet are hurting, let alone walk.

APRIL

1st April 1997 – Keswick

Tim and I have just parted on the bridge and I've walked back to Braemar, all the time becoming aware of the immense pain in my chest. I really don't know what to write right now. A lot has been discussed most deeply and there's no immediate major move on the cards.

In essence I'm confused and scared still, but about different aspects of fully accepting responsibility for my life, my body.

Nothing's changed the way I feel about Tim, I still love him totally and want to spend a lifetime together wherever and whenever that may be. I have thought about making love to T before but in reality . . . obviously I'm attracted to him and it's because of who he is – it's not driven by lust. Lust is easier, lust driven love falls into pigeonholes more easily. Fucking hell. Can't take it in and make sense yet. Love hurts. It's often a sharp pain or a dull hollow ache for the missing part. A longing you can't describe but you know it's there.

2nd April 1997 – Dallinghoo
Well, it's well and truly gone to shit this evening. I know I need to move out: Mum's feeling claustrophobic, Mike's moving in in a month and they want their space. To be honest I feel like I'm infringing on their lives when I shouldn't be. There are times that it hasn't felt at all comfortable here. So tomorrow I'll take responsibility and find somewhere else to go, even if it's just short time until I find my own place.

7th April 1997
Today I've seen an aromatherapist who gave me some Reiki healing. The healing was different to any I've experienced before. I saw images, there were eyes, like a third eye and pyramids, a sphinx, very dark then a seagull swooping, lightning flashes, an underwater tank. I stood watching a turtle swim. She touched my left foot and a flash of ice blue appeared to the far right, again it came, aqua out of an eye socket, the face reflecting was my own looking back at myself, more flashes of blue. This blue then became green and both colours appeared together, still from an eye.

Felt most strange afterwards, unearthly, stupid – like slow brain and reaction. Calming, although I kept brimming with tears, not sure exactly why? She also mentioned that I may have problems with Candida and Gluten.

11th April 1997

Spoke to Tim this evening and he's, well, he doesn't think he could handle me moving to Keswick because of him. Basically I've an interview at Brysons that has live-in accommodation, so if I'm offered it, then what? I've a carer job here now as well. I have to think about what I really want to do. I can take the job in Keswick and start afresh, make new friends, contact with people, a room to live in and beautiful surroundings OR stay here and get on with care work, concentrate on nursing, move to Felixstowe and walk away from Tim and immerse myself in it.

But on the other hand, if I don't get living in Keswick out of my system I may regret not trying it while the opportunity is there. This is a hard decision. It seems the closer we get to dreams the more they dissolve.

My thoughts on Keswick are that of course I'd like to be near T but not to exert pressure, just if he wants to see me you know I'm there. I'll be working 90% of the time and maybe this is the only way I can face up to life, to looking after myself, to hold down a job. It all entails independence because there will be no one to depend on except me. Scary stuff, hey?

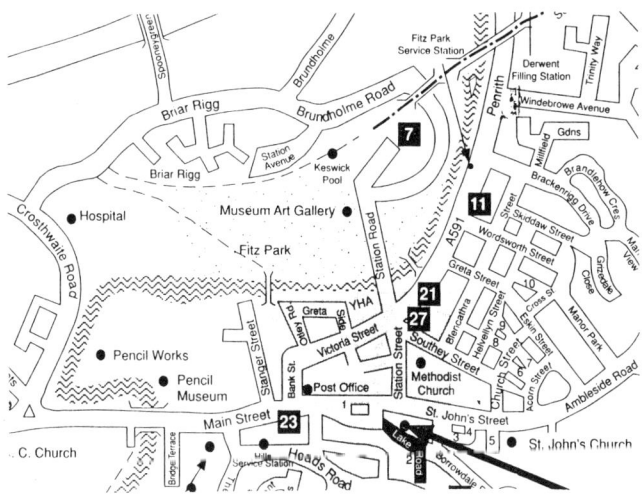

MAY

3rd May 1997

WELL ching, ching, all change. I am indeed in Keswick, got a room, got a job, getting a life! Life can be strange. I came up a couple of weeks ago for an interview and ended up being offered two jobs and decided on the receptionist one. SO . . .

I've seen T a couple of times and he's annoyed that I undermined him by blatantly moving to Keswick against his wishes. But what can you do, the more I'm told not to do something I may actually want then this strange kind of strength and determination kicks in.

My depression has lifted, anxiety reduced, obviously there is still an element of being unsettled and the odd food related panic which I'm trying to keep controlled. Essentially though, things are better, a real element of peace is present. I'm in awe of the beauty that surrounds me.

I saw *Romeo and Juliet* last night and blubbed away as well. Things are going to be OK, I can make this work for real.

10th May 1997

On my days off I have spent most of the time sleeping. It's been an odd week. Wednesday was totally shitty, felt worse for wear from drinking and the horrible rash covering my legs. Have also felt very insecure at work and unbelievably scared of losing my job. The problem is that I really want this to work out and I just don't want to cock it up. I've been picked up on my appearance and my uniform. I am trying to make sure I'm presentable but I feel undermined and it has knocked my confidence in my ability.

Oh, and the main problem, mixed with the drink, I binged BIG TIME and it fucked me up both physically and mentally.

15th May 1997

From tomorrow I AM going to start eating properly and not feast on sugar etc. These past three days I've just eaten and eaten and eaten, not felt hungry but have carried on. Today I thought I'd got it sorted but since dinner it's gone to shit. I've crammed to capacity in the last hour. I feel very bloated and have put on weight. I can feel it, this worries me because I'm not eating properly.

I'm bingeing because I feel a sense of loss, rejection. Can't explain it exactly.

16th May 1997

Been having quite sexually confused dreams which always begs the question: if I had the chance, I would.

17th May 1997

Spent a lovely evening with Tim. We walked and talked, well I seemed to talk a lot, trying to explain the mess I'm getting myself into or rather out of. I also admitted I was attracted to him, it's only recently it's clicked. I remember seeing him one day on my way home from work and I just thought I am really attracted to him.

18th May 1997
I feel mentally tired and on a short fuse. Work beckons soon and I am not in the mood for putting up with any hassle.

STRESSED, TEARFUL, ON EDGE, UNSTABLE

20th May 1997
VIOLENCE, its physicality, is maybe something some people need in their relationship. (I wonder why I have such cravings for sweetness, the urge to gorge and feed on these foods until I'm dizzy, sick and bloated).

JUNE
1st June 1997
Once again I've made changes to my lifestyle, having left my job for a variety of reasons including their displeasure at me having gastric flu and needing time off!!! Also it was just getting too fucking stressful, so as of today I'm living and working elsewhere. The accommodation is grim and you have to share, but it's a roof over my head so I'm approaching it with my adaptable head on! So far so good. I'm working in Housekeeping. Today is the first day and it is pretty physically demanding but as long as I eat well then I shall cope. Our meals are provided, which is good. These two days I have eaten stuff that I haven't touched for a long, long time.

It's all out of my hands now, I just have to get on with things.

3rd June 1997
I wish I could explain to you my fears about body image, the

irrationality, the complexity, the misconceptions and worries. It's like I like being slim but am still too scrawny by far, my hands look so large against my tiny arms and compared to the others here I am childlike thin. I'm eating anything and tonight have gone over the top in a comfort feast. Yet I worry that all the chips, sausages and fat they're serving are going to stodge me. I'd rather get heavier through decent, healthy and varied meals: but what can I do, it's there so I eat it.

The hardest thing is feeling myself, becoming a physical presence with shape, having a bottom that creases, thighs that rub. No doubt I shall adapt because there is no other way forward but to grow and become strong. If I could snap my fingers and be at that stage I would. You know, it's the in-between phases that are here to test and teach.

SELF LOVING NOT SELF LOATHING

7th June 1997

God I've binged big style and this has to stop. I don't know what else to do except eat. From tomorrow no more chocolate, cakes, sweets, biscuits etc. until I've stabilised myself.

It's now 12.15 a.m. and I've come to the conclusion that I am very unhappy tonight and that is why I have done, am doing, this food abuse. Why is it I always return to it, yet I no longer starve, instead I gorge.

JULY
2nd July 1997

This morning I feel very good about myself, almost radiant! Met Tim after 12 and we took a bus to Kendal. It's been so lovely spending time together, sharing the time, scenery, thoughts.

Today I am settled. There were ideas of moving on possibly to Scotland but at the moment I'm quite happy with Keswick, life, work and living, so for now I'm going to enjoy what's happening here.

7th July 1997

I went round to see Tim last night. I was feeling very strange and uneasy but we had a good long chat about a myriad of things and I've got to find it in myself to tell Ian H. EVERYTHING on Wednesday.

T says it all falls into place now, I gave away the missing piece. The problem is I'm still not being honest with myself. I won't and don't acknowledge how events, experiences REALLY affected me. I just say I've dealt with it and I'm fine.

A lot of what's troubling now is self image, but it does run deeper into the realms of sexuality, sexual and creative power. It's so inextricably linked, it's such a driving force and was always essential to my being but now it frustrates and the energy scares me because I don't know how to use it without bouncing off the walls, becoming restless, agitated and uneasy.

8th July 1997

Today has been odd, a lot of negativity that I've had to battle against and it's most challenging. I'm fine, then shrouded, it lifts and you know, comes and goes! Also felt physically not on top form since Monday, mainly I'm just feeling quite bloated and curdled in the stomach, abdominal area.

Other thoughts . . . my mind is on tomorrow and finding the words I need to make my truth tangible.

10th July 1997

Much has happened and become confused since yesterday. I saw Ian H. and that was cool, so 2 weeks from now we'll make a start. Spent yesterday with Tim, he dyed my hair, we walked, talked and he's in a dilemma about moving away now we're getting on so well. It was a lovely few hours though, peaceful, relaxed, then came back here and ended up drinking quite a bit with everyone, good fun. Later on I told Col I was attracted to him and I didn't run, well not too much. I was kind of cold and a tad unresponsive because I didn't want things to go too far. I kept thinking I should be enjoying this more. Maybe I just don't do empty fucks.

Hence there is much inner turmoil, not helped by the fact I only got 2 hours kip and was still drunk this morning. I'm glad it happened because at least it means I'm making a start on confronting and overcoming my problems with sex, intimacy, emotion. I keep thinking about this possible situation with Jason too!

12th July 1997

Yesterday was so good, there was sun. I wore the yellow dress Charlie helped me buy in Stoke. Went to Penrith and then in the evening off into town for drinks. The most major thing that's happened today is between me and T. I popped round to see him and I don't know how this came up but I said I'd like to go out with him, it got very serious. A lot of intense staring and when I looked into his eyes I felt and I saw being in love, being together. We didn't kiss. I can't believe how much I wanted to, I seemed amazingly calm (unlike T), I guess because it seemed so natural. This new honesty policy is pretty dangerous; stuff is coming out of me that is surprising, it's another side that's coming free and forward. With Tim I actually had emotion, I could sense being in love and it's taken 18 months of friendship, flirting and confusion to suddenly over the past few weeks behaving as adults and honesty, then bang, it hits us square on.

In the past 3 days I've experienced more than I have in years and it's all to do with emotions, testing out what's me and what's not me and I'm taking it in my stride. The boundaries are getting relaxed, the walls smaller, my needs are being recognised though there are still elements of denial but it's early days: it's better to try than remain safely at a distance desiring but never participating in life.

Thank you and goodnight!

13th July 1997

I awoke to the wonderful sound of rain splattering on leaves. The air is slightly relieved from suffocating stuffiness. Well . . . Tim called just before 7 and I've been there most of the evening. It's been intense and strange, a mass of emotion, we've also kissed each other and that was good; it didn't make the situation any clearer. We've decided we are partners and are embarking on a relationship of some description based on total honesty. This is the one rule, to be completely honest, so if the way we feel changes we have to say so. Whoah, it's all kind of, this is going to take a while to sink in and get used to. I'm excited, nervous, happy, glowing. Kissing Tim, it's so different kissing someone you really feel for. We love each other for who we are, know we want to be together so now we're working out the best way to show it.

I can't believe all this has happened. In just a few days there's been so much coming out and last night and now. Things are changing; I'm changing becoming whole, more of a true self that's developed rather than been reconstructed. It's all happened so quickly. I'm so calm and accepting though, the positive thing is that we are both taking the risk, trying out this new way of being instead of denying, hiding, trying the here and now rather than the overall picture.

15th July 1997

A lot keeps happening. Last night I saw T who is deeply troubled by this new element to our relationship; he doesn't understand why it's suddenly come up and is finding internal pressures about how he should now behave towards me purely because of the way previous things he had with girls have gone. When I saw him I had already geared myself up for a fall as I half expected him to say, 'I can't cope with this, let's put things back to how they were.'

But Tim has said he'd have no problem saying that; it isn't what he wants. SO it's a case of him needing to face the underlying cause. I mean to be honest; I don't understand why but I've accepted it and I seem to have no major qualms with the situation. I just wish Tim was handling it better. When we were sat in the graveyard talking, inside I thought, shit, if anyone else was being like this I'd say fuck you and walk away, but with Tim I can't walk away.

All the times he's hidden from me, kept me at arm's length and been distant, I could never say I don't need a friend to treat me like this. WHY? It's got to be because I love him unconditionally and have never expected anything (that much I've learnt!) Sure, I've been hurt in the process, but have denied the pain.

16th July 1997

Yesterday I saw Mum for the first time in 3 months. It was great to be with her for a while and today she left for Troon and I just ended up crying, partly because I don't know when I'll see her again. There was a mass of emotion all swirling up. It's still there now because I'm tearful. Another thing is I feel like shit and am very tired and cold. Seeing Mum and Mike made me appreciate the fact I don't live with them any more because that was a pretty trying time for us all. I couldn't go back to it. I hope that I've shown how much I've come on, to reassure Mum, myself, that I'm finally pulling life together. AT LAST!

18th July 1997

I'm quite drunk and it's only 6.30! Anyway it's been a crazy day or so. Tim and I are now sorted, we're not seeing each other romantically any more, purely as friends. In a strange way I feel relieved. We walked up Latrigg last night and did much in depth talking. I love him regardless. You know what it's like when you smell an item of clothing and breathe them in, that's what it's like.

It's better to have a strong friendship than a teetering relationship.

Still the night is young and once turndowns are over, it's time to hit Keswick.

19th July 1997

Stu's just left and I feel seriously tearful. I'm going to miss him. Chris has gone too, we had a hug as he was getting very tearful this morning. It's strange how attached you can become even though I've only known them 7 weeks.

Sunday 20th July 1997

It's been a long day, have felt very tired and a little depressed too but at least I have tomorrow off once turndowns are done. Also had Tim in my thoughts. Man, I'm just fed up with a lot of things, namely the fact I've OD'd on sugar, drink and am eating shit thus am rundown. FUCK YOU.

It's late. I stood on the porch in the cool night air, staring at the full moon boldly illuminated against the deep blue sky and was swamped by an intense feeling of being totally alone.

Monday 21st July 1997 (6st 10lbs)
A bad night full of nightmares, a plastic baby called Magda, Ian killing his ex-girlfriends, National Express coaches, an old teacher, my brother, all mixed up and confusing. Awoke just after 6 a.m. restless, tired, so got up, got out. Gloriously hot, bright day.

Fucked off, no, pissed off, with my weight. Shit, in the last week I've eaten more biscuits, sweets, cakes etc. etc. and drunk loads more alcohol but have lost 4 fucking pounds. WHY? This could explain why I'm feeling so wretched. I have to stop this sugar feeding, it's depressing me. This is like a real low. Other thoughts . . . I wish I was in Cornwall right now and able to see Dad.
VERY LOW SELF ESTEEM TODAY

23rd July 1997
Today I've seen Ian H. Man, he cuts straight through any bullshit and intellectual rationalisations and I like that. He sees through the shit and confronts what I can't vocalise or feel that I can't allow myself to acknowledge or need. Why don't I allow the honesty to want, need or desire? Am I that afraid of being hurt or does the truth scare me. I cried a couple of times when he asked me about Dad and then when we talked about Tim. He says that from what he sees we are a couple already; we may not realise it yet but it's obvious. He also wants Tim to come along at some point.

That's the thing, he sees my intelligence and thinks I have very slanted views and standards towards people and life. Ian's the first person I've seen in this field that I haven't felt the need to be on guard and play them at their own game. I can tell him as much as I consciously know and the rest he'll find and help me to realise. This is why I can't flit away now, this holds me because the opportunity to confront the truth is here and it has to be done. It's what has to be focused on NOW.

25th July 1997

I'm fucked bigtime, all these emotions are coming out that I don't want to feel because it hurts too much. At the moment I want to drink myself into oblivion, cliché I know but . . . Tim's told me he's moving away in a month's time which will be hard. It seems the closer I get to being, the further away my dreams fall. That's why if you never want then disappointment is easier to handle and dismiss, but right now I am in real pain, so much emotion is running riot and my defences are down. It's not at all comfortable. It's like Tim, I love him and want to be with him, in fact I wanted to kiss him, but I know it's not right for him so I should forget it. I can't though, because that's not being honest.

Fucking hell, it's all a mess. I have a deep foreboding that when Tim goes that'll be it. I feel so silly, so weak for wanting to be with him. In a way I feel he's running from the situation and I don't know if I can keep following or even if I should. FUCK! FUCK! FUCK! I am so alone on this earth and in so much pain, it's draining my life and leaving me melancholy.

26th July 1997

Last night I can't believe how much I cried. I lay there with my headphones on and just wept for ages.

29th July 1997

Yesterday was strange, scary and quite nice. Felt dizzy, headachy and sick so only worked until 12 then went to bed for a few hours and ate and ate etc. Went to T's, bass in tow. Very panicky at that point because I was feeling uncomfortable and craving chocolate, junk food. Tim was cool though, played a few tunes, it kind of calmed me. Went and got BOUND (gave into cravings bigtime). It was lovely just watching a film, messing about, relaxed and ended up staying over. Slept beautifully, only woke once at 5.30, then slept until 10.45! A strangely peaceful deep sleep filled with warmth and dreams.

Today I completed my first canvas type thing in many years.

31st July 1997

Phoned home. Cheap wine. Rain. Feeling like a cripple crappled old body, fragile and achy. Must be the weather . . .

AUGUST

1st August 1997

There seems to have been a lot to think about. Last night there were many mixed up dreams involving work, Tim and strange but oddly familiar surroundings. I awoke briefly after the part with T because it seemed very real. Basically we'd just been lying in bed together when he made a move, so we're kissing very intensely and as we moved on further he suddenly pulled away and went cold on me. He said, 'Admit it, you want me.' And I lay there trying to deny it: 'I don't want you because I know I can never have you.' Very soul destroying dream! But maybe true, acting out what's happened but in a different setting.

Was also screaming at some strangers to get the fuck out of my place because it was mine and I wanted to be left alone. Then there was family and my Mum's friends having a go at me when I tried to slink away. FUCKED. Big thoughts have been about my family, why I've been so distant and then there's Ian as well. So there's been sleep, feeling physically steamrollered and weak. Rain.

3rd August 1997

Today's shit, my head's shit. Am incredibly insecure and scared. Had a chat with T after work trying to find out why, but I'm such a mass of confused thoughts and hurt that it's hard to be honest any more. My defence mechanisms kicked in most spectacularly after I broke down crying, then zing, I pulled myself together and became emotionally cold and empty. You know T and I have both regressed in dealing with each other, we've both fallen back since the time we kissed. Our last moment of true honesty was on Latrigg (2 weeks back). Since then I've denied what I thought was natural and wanted, in case it's too much for Tim; I can't face rejection, hurting, but I already am so it's fucking pointless. He kind of realises all this and says the only way for us to be adult is for me to honestly admit how I really feel about the situation, about what I want, wanted, and then on his part he'll oh . . . so there's much turmoil because of denial but I don't know what to do. We've got to get back to an adult level because right now it's pure need, I'm so insecure. I physically need Tim in a truly unhealthy way. If I don't get back to a stronger level before he leaves it's just going to be fucking stupid and I will find it intensely difficult.

Everything's coming through in my dreams and I can't run from them.

Am most depressed and huh . . .

Seeing Ian H. is bringing up so much stuff that it confuses because I'm not entirely sure what's surfacing or how to deal with it properly. My defences aren't so good anymore, feelings keep slipping through and stinging. So far it seems to be pain related to those I love and who maybe I didn't get as much love from or the kind of love I've needed; that's not necessarily through them withholding though, it's a mixture of how it was shown, whether I acknowledged it or pushed myself further away.

Basically, if I could see him weekly it'd be more support,

because it gets confusing and I can't seem to deal with everything, it's being very destructive right now.

5th August 1997

The atmosphere between Laura and me sucks. We've barely spoken to each other for days . . . I know I've not been very responsive of late because my head's in a mess and I'm withdrawing. It's not paranoia. Am I that difficult to live with?

Danger signs are showing again, thoughts of going into a clinic are rife. On the one hand it's better to live a normal life and sort things out as I go along but I know while I have 100% control there's always a safety net to fall back into. I could stay stuck in this rut forever if I don't regain my weight and clear my mind, SOON. Right now I'm scared and insecure, tired of life. My vision has become narrowed, anything peripheral is of no consequence, no interest. I'm barely speaking, turning in on myself. It's waiting in the wings.

I guess the other thing that has made a major impact on me today is receiving a photo of Mum and me together. I didn't even recognise myself at first glance. Looking closer scared me intensely. I seemed so meek, scared eyes and physically . . . why can't I be a woman? What will be so terrible about being real, finding myself in an adult form? You see all this turmoil is too much to take. I can't stand 24 hour conflict much longer without caving further. I need help and I need it now. I am so aware that if I was living alone I couldn't care for myself and feed myself properly which is crap. So where is the progression? In some ways I'd come so far, changed attitudes and ideas to life but still haven't learnt to care for myself and that is such a key element and it needs confronting.

Oh, my head hurts.

Can't sleep and have just killed loads of baby flies that came crawling out of the ceiling. I deserve more than this, I'm living in a shithole, riddled with damp, bugs, and smelly. My quality of life sucks. I hump myself round housekeeping, eat shit staff meals and share a room. There is no sanctuary to find peace or sanity as you always have someone else to consider. Sometimes I don't mind, it's a case of survival, but things need to change.

Also spoke to Laura and she's moving rooms, so suspicions confirmed. Apparently it's not because I'm a bitch to live with, it's that we're too alike. Is she being honest? Before we felt like friends and now it's just we share a room, total distance, fucked up.

Compared with times I've had before this, now is a better life than I've lived for a long while.

6th August 1997

It's 11.30 p.m. and I've pigged out on several portions of chocolate cake and Fanta! A kind of desperation set in. I always resort to eating shite. Anyway, all that is beside the point (it's probably a guilt thing that made me write that). I've seen Ian H. and put forward the need for me to have more help i.e. a clinic. He rang up a nurse at a Penrith unit and they have a bed free so all I need to do is go for an assessment then I could be admitted. I'm shit scared because if they say sure we'll give you the bed, I'm entering into something that's alien but may be an experience I have to go through in order to come out complete. My anorexia is staring me in the face and it's trying to get another grip as my strength has deteriorated, the will to fight is weak. It's a prime time for it to take advantage. Thus preventative measures are top priority. Apparently he was going to tackle me about my weight this week but I beat him to it.

How do I explain this to my boss without making it sound like I'm fucked up? Where to start . . .?

Enveloped

Thursday 7th August 1997

Finally spoke to Mum and she's 100% behind any decision I make. She also sent me a gorgeous bouquet which made me all emotional. I've spoken to my boss and she is amazingly good about me potentially going into hospital. I was up all night stressing. It's cool though.

My assessment isn't until next Thursday which seems so far away. I'd hoped for tomorrow. I'm impatient and need it now. I just hope I can convince them to take me in because if they don't all my hope will be gone. It's hard to contemplate continuing this way. I am so scared of the consequences of being left to my own devices: destruction and deterioration lie in wait. I am weak.

Sounds dramatic but it's honest. All I can do is be honest.

Friday 8th August 1997

It's been so hot and weakening this weather. I want to keel over and jack it all in. Tim turned up at mine this evening, obviously after seeing my note. He's concerned and doesn't think hospital is the right place for me, I can do this alone, but he doesn't see the desperation I face, a third relapse in 8 months and it's going to keep me at this point until I seriously do something. I am scared but see I have to relinquish control. I'm desperate. After tomorrow my next day off isn't until Thursday, maybe it's better to keep busy but . . . He puts my current backtrack down to the fact us going out didn't come to fruition and thinks if he was staying etc., I'd be OK. It's not that simple.

My eyes are opened, I see stuff I'd been kidding myself about clearly, the shithole I live in, the job, the way I treat myself and others. Also Tim and I are just not going to happen. I had to come here though, work out what Keswick held, it's been a positive move, I've worked, lifted the majority of depressive thoughts and changed attitudes to some degree. Tim thinks weight isn't the issue, it's how you feel, which is true to a point but not when you're probably . . . 7st (?) have the body of a teenage girl and no periods. My hip bones are protruding more and my hands seem larger against the thinning wrists.

This is the body I want to stay trapped in? NO, no fucking way. I know weight as weight isn't the issue but it's necessary to be healthy, feel attractive, solid. The eating, the way I abuse food is one key. I can eat but not sensibly, properly, it's erratic, bingeing, using it to fill my time and my mind.

My level of rational clear thought is blurring, even simplistic things make my head hurt.

I'm trying to keep the panic at bay, it's not easy, especially when I'm alone, all the thoughts of what I could eat to take my mind off the problems, the waiting. It's so selfish and consumes.

It's growing dark and I'm in the park with Latrigg and Skiddaw at my feet.

Saturday 9th August 1997

Slept until lunchtime, very deeply. Saw a paper at Tim's, reports of Emily's last moments, how she'd clung to the mast screaming. It's an image I can't remove. I'd always hoped she'd died peacefully but she knew, saw the terror, swept away.

I'm much calmer now and determined that hospital is the right intervention for now. Basically I'm trying to gather myself together, remain calm and stable. If I was 6st and a jibbering wreck I'd have no problem getting the bed. I pray it's still free for me.

Be positive, accept the fear and use it to get what you need; the motivation, the will is there, it just needs tapping in the right environment to secure progress. I think I'm still stuck at the age of my anorexic onset. There's no doubt I know. So much is flowing, thoughts intercutting the calm. I see it staring back. In disgust I recoil from the mocking and its presence.

It is 10 to 12 and the urge to binge is upon me. I've grazed all evening and am full but sadly empty in other ways. There is so much noise and all I want is to hide in sleep.

Sunday 10th August 1997
Here comes another promise, from tomorrow I'll try to eat properly. I keep picking, chaotically, guiltily. My stomach is upset from the sugar feeding. It's almost like I'm scared to stop eating and I let myself down once and it goes crazy. It has been a bad day on the negativity front, I can't even pretend to smile. I can't be bothered with anything, feel no pleasure out of life, no taste. Toast, sugar and chocolate is where I return to. Basically it's depression.

Monday 11th August 1997
What a day, mixture of panic, scared. Weighed myself and I'm 6st 10, not good. So tired and weak right now, not sure if I could keep going. So instead have got drunk to obliterate the bad feeling. So frightened, can feel thoughts of eating rife in my mind. Plagued and afraid. Need sleep, rest . . .

Tuesday 12th August 1997
Made it through another day, bingeing feelings are rife but I'm trying to fight them. Getting drunk has helped clear my head but I'm aware that I have a false sense of being able to cope alone. Today has been quite easy compared to the past few. I'm feeling very bloated, uncomfortable and heavy.

Still agitated and restless underneath the exterior.

Isn't body distortion strange, how the thinner you get the more bloated and difficult you feel, especially my stomach, the most sensitive area; it always has been and I know as I gain it'll cause stress. It's all so stupid. Then reality snaps in, you feel the hip bones jutting, ribcage and spine showing, enormous hand against a tiny wrist. Not having a full length mirror I only ever see sections, not the full picture. I am never whole, always fragmented, distanced. Sometimes I kid myself I don't look so bad but when I look into my hollow eyes the horror is clear.

I hate to obsess about all this and be so inwardly focused but I have to make this a positive priority. I want to know why I abuse food this way, whereas for others it's just essential, they take it and walk away. I haven't stopped eating or drinking but remember sensations, a revulsion of not wanting to put anything inside your mouth. In a way it's that battle that forces me to eat, to graze and binge because not eating isn't an option, it's the way, the what I eat, that's the problem.

Twilight thoughts, thoughts of the future, of friends, of Tim. Maybe this time I won't follow, once I'm out of hospital. I won't be second best and settle for less.

Wednesday 13th August 1997

Mum called, good chat and I meant to say things but I forgot. I keep forgetting because my head hurts. Confusing. Kath brought the hoover over, probing about tomorrow. I know people here probably suspect. She thought and asked if I was Bulimic. I kid myself I can get away with this lie but they see it everyday; the physical, the mental I hold together outwardly since I'm not in the position to indulge in letting it all hang loose otherwise I'd lose everything.

The fight is getting so tiring that I've had thoughts of OD'ing if all does not go well. It's pathetic I know but I'm that desperate I don't see how else to make them see I'm serious and crying out for help. I canna stand this no more, one way or another it has to stop.

Friday 15th August 1997 – Beacon Unit, Penrith Hospital

'God she's thin.' It's because I'm a fucking anorexic. Geez

don't you think I know that. Sat on the toilet, had a quick cry and pulled myself together.

Well, here we are, the Beacon Unit, Penrith Hospital. I'm scared, I'm scared, I'm scared. Weight's fucking dropped further to 6st 7. Lost 3 lbs in 4 days and it sucks. I want to hide in this room, I'm clinging for security. I feel so young and afraid.

FUCK I'M ANGRY! It's pulsing through my veins and I want to kick the shit out of someone.

Tim's been a star today.

Why do I have so much stuff? Everything seems so vital but I guess in a strange way it is, especially my art stuff. It's familiar and is me, the only sense I have of me.

So, day one on a . . . well a new battle to get better. I've been told I may leave before I'm totally recovered, a month maybe. I felt like disintegrating. I'm aware complete recovery could take time but I'm scared to go out alone if it's still lurking. Basically I don't believe I can do it in a month, a looming deadline. Today is a day for tears and I hurt physically, mentally I'm so tired.

Saturday 16th August 1997

Last night slept very sporadically. Got another mattress for the bed since it's so hard and hurts my bones. Legs kept going numb, stomach ache, vibrating head. Then slept 3 to 6ish, it wasn't restful, full of frets and scariness. Hence it's 8.30 a.m. and am very jaded, weak with a long day ahead to face.

Lunch was grim and all I can think about is cravings for sweets and chocolate.

I want sugar to lift my mood.

It's the end of the day and am definitely more relaxed and at ease with going beyond my room.

There is also the idea that I am currently not anorexic but rather suffering from a binge eating disorder which makes more sense. I promised myself I would never starve again and maybe this is the way I fight any lurking elements, I binge. I fight the fear inside by doing exactly what it doesn't want me to. I say FUCK YOU, I eat double that and more but that is destructive in its own way and not a very liveable coping mechanism. The problem is you see my frame and it says this is an anorexic body, it screams out to you but the head is predominantly not. In a way the bingeing is a need to prove I'm not, to let others see I do sit down and will happily eat. I will eat until I'm stuffed and panicky to prove I can eat. Eating disorders are all so fucked up but tonight I feel positive and a little more alive.

Sunday 17th August 1997

Slept well. Created in clay but am tired after lunch and craving sugar, sweets, and cider would be divine, so instead have had chocolate and jam but the thoughts are still there because I want them, can taste the cool cider.

Actually made an effort to bath today and put something clean on, sometimes it's easier not to then you don't have to think. This afternoon and evening has been so fucking hard, totally plagued by thoughts and the desire to drink and possibly binge. I have no coping strategy as I always end up indulging.

Monday 18th August 1997

Intense stomach ache which makes me feel uneasy.

Am wearing my lovely yellow dress to try and brighten my vision. It's sunny and I'm on the window ledge listening to PJ Harvey. Have the urge to go and have a manic dance about in the grass as I feel I'm about to bounce off the walls.

I want to go to the pub, the NEED got pathetic so I went to my darkened room and slept for 2 hours. Strange, lucid dreams, one involved me and Barbara entering a warehouse and there was a massive concrete incline covered in sand that we had to scramble up so we linked arms and just ran at it, even though the sand kept making us slip but we just ran harder and reached the opening which was a tube station leading onto a football pitch. Paul and Russell were chatting near the entrance but didn't see me. We ran onto the pitch to get across but the players kept coming our way so we decided to get on the path and walk round, arms and hands held. Sounds like one of those deeply significant dreams.

In an earlier one though, I was in pyjamas, slipping on a polished floor in a shopping centre, eventually I couldn't stand so just lay there being pushed by people's feet until I hit a big plant, then this hulking Russian guard appeared shouting at me. I couldn't understand so cowered. He then got out a snooker cue to beat me with, I grabbed it, snapping it which made him worse and more determined. I was saying, 'I'm from hospital, help me to bed.' I curled up in protection and his eyes glowed with glee as he got ready to enjoy what was coming next. Then poof, I awoke from phase one.

I'm not finding any comfort in food and I hate it.

11.30 p.m. and am in need of chocolate and coke to help me sleep, have already had some toast and more biscuits but it just doesn't satisfy the urge. I can have coke but not the chocolate so what's the point? I'm just taking my frustration out on the food as it's not . . . I'm not getting the buzz I need any more and everything is bland, uninspiring. Man, it's all so stupid and warped. Binges are a way of life, sugar is my treat, drinking is a pleasure (most of the time). Without these I am lost.

Have just taken the stinking tablet. I am better than tablets which is why I don't want anti-depressants. If I have to go through something I have to feel it not hide behind a mask. I've been dead inside for too long. Face not fake, but right now, AMY YOU ARE WEAK, a little white pill is taking your night away.

Enveloped

Tuesday 19th August 1997

It's been a most strange day. Clung to the sink and hauled myself off the floor to wobble round for breakfast, head banging, spacey, dead. Back to room and keeled over on bed until ward round. Tried to speak but couldn't do it, couldn't form words clearly, my tongue felt enormous, jaw disengaged, cabbaged. Lunch came and could only manage a few mouthfuls as I couldn't grip properly and as I brought the fork to head I kept blacking. Just felt nauseous, physically weak and in pain. I didn't really know what was what, trapped in a weak body and spaced out head. Having said that I'm more together now, still a bit woozy. Is it the sleeping pill wearing off? Strange, strange, scary too.

Needless to say I've not bathed or anything, it'll keep though.

Reality calling Amy, come in flaky chick! Others here go home for leave to reintegrate into a sense of normality but where is the normality to return to when I go? I have to create yet another scenario to live in.

I need to rethink my thinking so that it makes sense. I consider the future and am lost as sometimes, well 90% of the time, I can see no further than the state I have struggled in. After talking to Karen this evening she has enlarged my vision of regaining ground in the outside world, since if I'm 100% honest I don't want to go back to Keswick, chambermaiding, the chalets, living that way. I know Mum has said I could come home and set up in Suffolk but realistically that is too hard and not appropriate as I wouldn't get any follow up care. She suggested a flat in Penrith. The only thing that worries me about living alone is my habit of withdrawing. Living in Penrith has potential, though.

20th August 1997

There is a great unease since I don't know what to do with an upsurge of sexual power. I guess that's what makes a fully functioning body a daunting prospect.

117

8.45 a.m. and in panic, want to binge bigtime, need calming before I self destruct. Angry. Sat in the bath contemplating the pros and cons of being a corpse. I could picture the decomposing flesh hanging. Totally morbid.

PROS AND CONS OF BEING A CORPSE. I become a skeleton, no feelings, no basic human needs to attend to, peace, complete denial; when you're dead nothing can harm you and loss of potential that I denied because I'm too scared to fulfil it.

I could walk out of here and fuck off and die somewhere. I think the main road has potential, a nice bridge to teeter on until the pathetic drive in self pity pushes me to it. When I lived in Trimley, the bridge always had potential, you'd stand mesmerised by the thundering sounds of trucks rumbling beneath you, watching them whizz by and realise how easy it would be. I had climbed to the other side and clung on one night but the fear of becoming a bloody mass to be scraped, unrecognisable from tyres and tarmac formed an image that disturbed more than death.

I'm wallowing in self pity and guilt, there are many people in more dire situations than I. I feel I don't deserve help since I've brought all this upon myself.

Today I want answers to questions I'm not ready to face but the demand is there, muddling what feeble thoughts remain. The need to push until exhaustion is upon me, not physically just mentally, it's saying, 'Go on, fuck yourself up bigtime, you've got nothing to lose.' Fine except fucking sanity.

Why, why have I become this way? It's insane, destructive, selfish, conniving, fearful, hateful, critical, SAD. It seems like anorexia has been one big experiment. As I got into it I just tried different ways to nurture it. It's like sex, I wanted to experience as much as I could.

Maybe I don't want to get better.

Promazine to calm . . . More promazine at 6.15 as severe binge need set in, relaxed for a while but it's now 8.30 and the urges have set about uncontrollable urges so have gobbled toast, biscuits, dry cereal and some chocolate syrup all because I want a pack of sweets and I thought I'd get through it without them.

My guts hurt, the Senakot hasn't kicked in yet so am in much discomfort and unease. I sense the days are getting harder and I'm not prepared for it. I can't just take a pill every time panic sets in.

I wish I was happy.

21st August 1997

Took half a Tamazepan to induce sleep, it felt good as it kicked in, like when you've had too much to drink and you're trying to remain upright then bash, you just go. This morning though, I am dipping between being wired. I feel as though I have the stares and am a little weary, wary of everything around me. It took three attempts to get up as sleep kept catching me again.

It's a battle of wills today. I need to find a singular form instead of this splitting. I am not the Amy that was intended, instead I am two, neither of which bears resemblance to the truth.

They are extremes.

I think I'm functioning normally, normally in my scheme of things and am being clipped here but it's because I'm used to having to keep going and going regardless of what is real inside. I have to deny the truth to remain strong. But they recognise the limits of thought, rationality, I still can't ask to talk. I didn't speak to anyone about what was running through my mind yesterday and I wanted to but . . . all I managed was to get tablets to quell the binge urge.

Missing pieces keep appearing or are from other puzzles. The picture isn't clear and I am sure there is more masked underneath. As though it was completed once, reprinted over to create another but what was left before is fragmenting through, two images in one piece, blurring the clear, indistinguishable.

I must brush my teeth, my mouth tastes rank. See, my mind is flitting from thought to thought and I have to catch them quickly before they're lost. Hot, bothered and deeply unhappy. I don't like my body and I don't like myself. This is pure self hatred.

Have been out in the rain and it was lovely to feel it on my skin but was brought back in again. I only wanted to feel something nice for a change, something natural.

Have talked this evening and was totally honest. This is the happiest I have felt, my mood is lifted and I feel quite bouncy. I am definitely going to take the anti-depressants since if my current trend of low mood continues everything will get harder and worse, it's just another way of anorexia trying to regain control. Yet my provocative side is excited about the prospect of owning and experiencing a full body.

22nd August 1997

Only slept for 3 hours but have awoken alive and dare I say happy? I'm surrounded by a sense of relief, a lifting mood. Have bathed, cleaned up room and generally making the effort. The positive side is winning through but it does leave me with false ideals as to my current state. Ask me now and I'll reply, 'I'm fine, feeling good,' but it ain't the truth, just another extreme. I'm either up, down and a lot of the time disinterested and lethargic.

Feelings of strength and defiance. Positive defiance as I have to show I am serious and can progress. Also think I may have gained a little weight in the past week or could it just be that I don't feel as fucking rundown as when I arrived, stopped bruising too, so things are looking up.

1 p.m. and am suddenly hit by tiredness, my shins are in pain and ache. Head is a bit bleary.

What do I know about myself? For definite I am intelligent, talented, creative and strong. In fleeting moments I consider myself attractive, sexual, approachable.

What I deny? The natural course of progression (evasive answer or what!!!) Seriously though, becoming part of our family, becoming a woman in all senses, needs, desires, ambitions, other people entry into my life. It's a case of denying and fighting against the above.

It's 10.50 p.m. and am in bed. I can't describe the intensity of the pain in my right shin, it's almost as though the bone there is hollow and knee joints are aching, shaky too. It's intense, impact and hurts like fuck basically. This used to happen an awful lot before and it's back again. It's a cripple, crappled old bones feeling. Am still happy though, despite this.

Also experienced a strange *déjà vu* moment with Karen earlier on. Several months ago I'd dreamt the scenario we were in and just as I was about to ask a question, it smacked me straight in the forehead, but how? How could I ever have known about this place? That stuff always seems to happen, it makes you wonder what the thought processes are that cause a sudden realisation of familiarity.

Fuck, my legs are cramping, yet again. Stop it, bastards. It's almost as though the shins are being injected and the fluid is creeping up, getting sharper, more acid as it travels through what was once marrowbone. A vice-like grip and like you've been beaten and kicked. Right, redirect focus.

23rd August 1997

It's 2.23 a.m. exactly, wide awake with tea and biscuits. Right leg cramped, cramping so bad I awoke from deep sleep. Discomfort and bloated. I need to give up my concave stomach and sculpted hipbones since they are more precious to me than I openly wish to acknowledge. I'll miss the inward curve that has been my reassurer. I've lost it once before and in a way came to love my stomach in its natural state. I don't believe the enormity of status it holds in the hierarchy of concerns, add that to the thighs, the sides, the flesh. It's all about control, can I control the emerging body? Essentially no, no I can't, it has to be allowed to grow. What needs to change are my mental attitudes and ideas towards it, adapt to the fear of feeling your thighs rubbing together, of them spreading when you sit – you know, the normal stuff that the other 90% of women feel everyday. Of course they may not be comfortable with it either but they haven't had to focus in and develop their neurosis so it takes over all common sense and reasoning.

24th August 1997

I'm excited about seeing Mum this morning. Here come the cows on a mission to munch. It's strange to think they'll end up on somebody's plate. I really do enjoy being here. It's the first time for years I've stopped; even when refeeding myself before I did rest but because I had so much mixed up shit in my head there was never any peace. Never any outlet.

I still feel remarkably happy and it's rather odd, obviously entering a good phase. Maybe it's because my determination to overcome is so strong. I'm enjoying it while it lasts which sounds pessimistic but I'm aware this is not the norm.

Today has ended being so hard. Been out with Mike and Mum and it's made me realise how fragile and ill I am. We'd only been in Penrith for half an hour or so and it was all so strange and shaky. Yet again my concentration is poor and my head hurts, nearly passed out at one point but was holding myself together for appearances sake.

Have touched an extremely raw nerve this evening, the connection being loss and the pain of it. How I can't let those who've died die, instead of purely seeing it as a separation, and what did happen that July 1986 in France that caused me to return a different girl? I don't remember even being there, maybe vaguely? That was the time we left Langer Road for Trimley. Once I start crying I can't stop. I feel the pain in the pit of my stomach, stabbing me. I find no comfort. You know I'm so insecure, in my surroundings, in myself. I don't want to become, or rather continue being, a danger to myself. HELL. Am emotionally tired and frightened of the way ahead. My relationship with Ian is the only time I have felt secure. I suppose there must have been security at an early age but stuff from so far ago, why are there no memories? I'm so old in many respects yet 24 is fast approaching and I am mistaken for a 16, 17 year old girl; it's hard to convince people otherwise when you present them with such a childlike image until they realise the old head that sits on these shoulders. I don't claim a wealth of experience or wisdom, just that I grew up too quickly, took on too many burdens, responsibilities, worries, concerns and secrets alone.

I can do this – I CAN GET BETTER.

Rash on my arse as well. Geez, I feel like a fucking hypochondriac, the bruising, the shin pains, the verruca and now rashes!

25th August 1997

4.39 a.m. (2 hours sleep) Woke up absolutely wet with sweat and stomach pains too.

Lots of thoughts about the future, I have considered living by the sea, artist option and also travelling. I love to create and if I could just do that it would be wonderful.

If I was given a choice, a chance to relive the past few years with the option to change any aspect of them, there is nothing I would omit, even my deepest, hellish, tormented moments. Anorexia has been obviously the most highly destructive aspect but I would never want to lose that because the whole spectrum of experiences have resulted in understanding or rather the beginnings of understanding and overcoming. In fact I view it as truly positive. To have lived without its impact, who can say whether life would be any better. Live through the shit and in comparison the rest will be a blast.

26th August 1997

Since I was 14 I've not eaten a balanced diet. Even then I'd go for cakes, sweets and chocolate as a replacement. It was never of any interest to me, food, and I remember saying, 'If I never had to eat it wouldn't bother me.'

The connection between eating and existing was, I don't know, I wouldn't think oh I've not had much today, I'd better get something else, there was always tomorrow. The only time I recall proper meals was when Ian and I were together. As I neared 17, 18 my body started becoming a problem. I'd worry about my stomach not being flat, I always felt tired, got bloated and had one thrush infection after another. Eventually it overtook.

Being with Ian was the only time I can identify being truly happy, I was in love, felt loved, the whole relationship was everything, he was my equal and I did neglect friends because Ian was number one in my life and I wanted to be with him as much as possible. He was my sanctuary from my family and yet I destroyed the thing which meant most to me. I cut myself away, got rid of things he gave me as I tried to deny it had ever happened as that was the only way I could cope with the immense loss that surrounded me. Maybe I thought if I'd never had it, denied it completely, then I could banish the pain away. Stupid fuck I am. I never told anyone how much it hurt or the fact I didn't want to end it but felt he didn't love or care for me as much, and my anorexic thoughts completely narrowed my sense of judgement. I was entirely trapped in depression, worthlessness and self hatred. Yet on the outside I was like . . . it's just one of those things, I still love him but . . . I was torn. No one could get in or even close. It demanded total isolation and I reciprocated these wishes.

I want to keep writing until my head fucking hurts and my body aches from the pain of feeling and finding the stuff I've hidden for so long.

Our relationship was the most constructive thing to happen to me, the most exciting and pleasurable too.

This is such a fucking relief to start really unloading these thoughts, they've been here for years and because they endlessly spin round I feel I've said this all before but it's never properly been vocalised. I've just heard it over and over, that's all.

This is a problem I have with Ian, I mean we're still friends but I don't know if he still wants me or whether I still love him, want him, because it's all been such a big mess. I think it's often better not to go back into things but it could have been the one constant relationship in my life if I hadn't let anorexia interrupt it. I never wanted anyone else, Ian was everything I needed and more.

That makes me so sad, overwhelmingly so.

Things are speeded up and it's hard to know what to pick up on first but whatever shit, no matter how insignificant I may feel it is, will be spewed on these pages. I'd be bingeing now if I wasn't here.

It's all very well writing but if you can't sort out the thoughts and feelings once they're out then you're fucked; that's when a binge begins as the sensations of panic and speed I feel inside are the same as the initial impetus that feeds the need to binge, just to take my mind away from what's there and concentrate on feeding cravings to divert feeling. I'm thinking about a Kit Kat now, that would start it off but I shan't. In fact I may test myself by buying a two finger one, eat it then walk away from what would usually ensue because I'm stronger than that, so much fucking stronger.

4.40 p.m. been asleep since 3, quite deep, awoke feeling shaky and still am, also very low, tearful, aching and exhausted. General stomach ache and discomfort. Right now I want to BINGE to forget the pain.

Tonight I don't want to sleep. It's now 12.50 a.m. Why won't I allow sleep? The less sleep I get, although beneath I'm tired, the more exhilarated I feel, the more manic and unstoppable.

So why fight the tablet?

26th August (or so I thought!)

Again I'm scared of being discharged before I'm ready. These insane thoughts of insecurity are rife, when I think this I feel out on a limb, alone and frightened because I know how much power I contain, how much destructive power, especially when my mind won't function rationally.

I want to cry out, 'I'm scared, I'm scared, I'm scared.' Once I'm out then there is going to be a lot to face and I need to be not only mentally but physically secure enough to stand my ground if it decides to have another go; if things are difficult, adjusting, then that's when it'll make its attempt.

Advantage anorexia, Amy – no love.

Whereas I want a treaty, an end to this battle. You've served your purpose, thank you so very much, so please LEAVE ME ALONE. I don't want to be one of those people who just manages an eating disorder so they can live with it, I want more than that. This companion who's been my enemy and my friend must be left behind but it's going to go kicking and screaming. It won't accept and give up without a fight. Amy wants to get better but the dormant anorexic Amy is saying, 'Fuck off, she's been happy these past few days in a row. She's fine like this.' I'm very torn. I WANT to be confined here until I'm really on top of this, while the anorexia is needing me to run because if I wanted to I could discharge myself but I won't. I WON'T. Stop kicking back at me. Let me find peace. Is this why I can't sleep fully? It doesn't want me to rest, it prefers a state of permanent torment.

I'm bruising again.

27th August 1997

Being abrupt, loud and authoritative does nothing to nurture the need to eat, it angers the anorexia into direct action which is always 'NO'. The stomach clamps down, the throat tightens and revulsion is all you feel towards the food, as if you put it in your mouth you'll fucking scream, not swallow.

Karen and I can talk to each other about our fears and experience because it's all so parallel. How can someone who's never had a problem with food understand the thoughts and feelings scattering your mind, swirling and confusing. I know if anyone else nags Karen I'm going to spit the dummy.

As usual it'll be misdirected as I'm sure it has only aggravated the dormant rage inside.

Where's it coming from?

28th August 1997

Bruising worse, red and angry looking, legs aching again, stomach upset.

This time of year always seems hard. This morning is bright but has an autumn edge to it. It was this time in 1993 that Ian and I split up and that I really became completely consumed by an anorexic lifestyle. I can feel it in my bones, in my body. Every year this happens, it's almost an indescribable sense of sadness that weighs upon my whole body and being. The emotions, the loss and emptiness is there, it's in me now and I'm becoming increasingly tired and achy. Head hurts. I want to curl up and forget. Yet my determination to get better is so strong, it's fighting through. I'm not here just to rest and put on a bit of weight, this is serious so there is no time to be complacent or arse about. I'm focusing on my goal and will go for it. Anything that stands in my way is going to get stomped down.

29th August 1997

The power I feel now is a driving force, headstrong. I always have been these things but they've been used destructively whereas now I'm turning the tables; but the new found feelings are quite overwhelming and today the power seems immense, almost unmanageable.

Could that be why panic is lurking? I'm very low, mentally tired and physically, physically sore.

Emotionally I feel quite cut off, not as perky as previous days. Apathy.

Sometimes I think all I have is what's left in my head. I want a drink. I don't want dinner.

10 minutes to go . . .

30th August 1997

Today I don't want to eat, it's so stupid, I am though, and what's inside doesn't like it one bit but that's why it won't allow me to taste or enjoy. BASTARD. I hate it, I HATE THIS FUCKING LIFE. I almost feel as though I've spent my whole life doing things other people want me to do. It's very rare that I've ever been true to myself as that's been construed as being stubborn! Maybe that's why I'm so glad to be cut off from the family while I sort my head out, I'm safe from having any visitors to confuse and make me put on an act. No need for pretence.

Walking around I see people, people who live in their bodies and use them. How do they do it? I feel apart from mine as though I live . . . no it's as though I'm merely the observer, while the limbs are controlled by something else. I wonder if they're really mine. Thought is the most destructive tool the mind possesses. I started too young and to think has been my downfall. My intelligence craved answers, knowledge, stimulation but grew bored so instead began to analyse all it saw.

There was so much noise moving past, as I in isolation wandered on. Weight, mass and flesh are in question. Once I really begin to feel myself, flesh against flesh, is when the trouble will begin, that's when anorexia will scream back in my face. I see it now. I sense many days of self hatred ahead as it despairs at the sensations and skin. As it is I hate myself, I hate my legs so beaten and bruised.

Do I hate myself or do I hate the anorexia? I'm so distanced from Amy, disengaged from her body. I must divorce the two, no divorce the three to find one.

Grow up, grow out, GROW AWAY.

SEPTEMBER

1st September 1997

Still agitated. Awoke at 2 a.m. and immediate urge was to binge. All I can think about is trying not to think about food. It's all so screwed up. Last night dreams were full of horror and pain, bingeing and starvation, shrivelled foetuses and mangled wombs, twisted ovaries and tubes. All in black and white. I think what I wish for is somebody to care for me, not because it's part of their job or because I'm their daughter, their sister etc. but because I am me.

2nd September 1997

No weight gain this week!!! I'm left wondering what's the point but am trying to turn the negative tide. Have been trying to think logically about a discharge plan, the pros and cons of Penrith and Felixstowe as they both have potential, but any decision I make could be more destructive than constructive. I am aware and scared of withdrawing. I could go two ways but it's having the bottle to commit to one thing and just hang on in there with it. It won't matter where I am if the anorexia decides to tempt me back. It just can't be allowed to. I can see if I can settle and stay with a decision and start doing something that fulfils my potential, uses my talents, I could feel so much better, even happy and the anorexia would fade merely leaving a stain.

VENLAFAXINE is being prescribed since I can't decide, to take or not to take.

6th September 1997

3 days of being disconnected, nauseous, shaky and sleeping. I have slept so much night and day, it's been a struggle to keep myself conscious and I've eaten so little because I've felt so sick.

I've already lost a lot of this week although I'm coming to now . . . It's 6 a.m. and I've been awake since 4 a.m. plagued by thoughts which keep looping but I'm almost scared to write them here because then they become real and I have to admit to them, they're words I don't know if I could say.

I destroyed my diary at the time to rid myself of the evidence; if it was never written, never acknowledged I could forget. Sometimes I wake and wonder what I'm doing here and whether I'll actually get any better than I am now if I can't unravel the past and let go.

8th September 1997

Help me, help me, help me. It's all gone to shit completely, just over 3 weeks of not bingeing fucked up. This morning panic is rife and I have gobbled. I still want, NEED MORE. I'm so stupid, pathetic and crap to make my stomach hurt more. I'd just like to drown myself in chocolate heaven, the cravings are so bad. My brain is totally switched off and am getting whatever

I can.

9th September 1997

Last night really was a total fuck up and I say from today I am taking a break from chocolate, sweets and so on because I am totally suffering, my head is binge groggy and stomach and sides are so sore that it hurts to sit, to breathe. I can't believe I used to make myself feel this bad every day.

Doubts are rife in my mind, what happens if I get out in the real world and don't like it! Have I the strength to make it mine? I can't face the thought of running, hiding again behind bingeing, behind food, behind eating, drink. I place my problems, my inability to cope in all these things.

10th September 1997

I almost feel a fraud as in what am I doing here, as the deep seated problems have submerged and I am dead inside and rather thin. So you see, it's all perfectly normal. I don't understand the food/weight/metabolism ratio, how the more I binged the more rapidly weight was lost. I don't understand, or rather don't think, anorexia has been lurking for years. Sure I was body conscious years ago but that never stopped me eating what I wanted, that only came at age 21. I never restricted my intake before. For years though I've suffered with stomach aches, abdominal pain, extreme tiredness, bloating, recurring thrush, limb pains, weakness, sore throats, a constant thirst. It's been put down to IBS and anything now is blamed on being anorexic, of course you'll feel this . . . because of the weight loss and so on. Of course your periods stopped . . . and I say BOLLOCKS to that one. They stop listening and only see the skeletal frame as blame. I'm sick of using eating disorders as an excuse for everything. I'm sick of doctors using it as an explanation. I'm sick of it all. It's just not good enough anymore, any of it.

I cannot blame having a lot to handle for my anorexia. That particular road was one I slipped into, almost unknowingly, rapidly it took hold. Rather than being helped, I was told I was obviously anorexic and off you go, so I grew into that label, it became an identity I fulfilled.

I DON'T UNDERSTAND ANY OF IT

12th September 1997
I'm sitting looking at the window, in my room, and thinking I am so lucky to be here but everything seems so half hearted and I lack interest, I'm in a sticking place. It's an illness that has no miracle cure and is rarely completely eradicated. I need a change inside my mind and only then will it make a difference.

13th September 1997
Existing as half person, I can't face that I'd rather be dead. I will never change until I learn to live with myself. As my brain function improves so will the memories.
Survive is all I ever fucking do, just survive.

16th September 1997
Where do I start? Been told it's time I became an out patient and have until the end of the week to find somewhere to live! She told me there are other people waiting to come in and if I'm going to treat this place like a hotel! What the fuck? Where did she get that idea from. No one said a word to back me up.
So I'm obviously perfectly healthy and 6st 9lbs is a good weight to live at! My eating disorder is of no consequence, it's all been addressed, one week for every year I've had it. Simple. I'm not worth the time, the input or the money. I gave up my job to do this, where I lived, and it is the only reason I stayed, to sort myself out. I knew I'd be discharged underweight and

132

unrecovered but not this far off from it and now I'm totally resigned to the situation.

Where have I gone wrong? Am I too happy, too positive at times. I've not allowed myself to be fed drugs and pacified like the rest. I don't kickback, don't dissolve into tears on the staff or have screaming fits, I eat my meals, follow the diet. How the hell am I supposed to let go when I've become so conditioned at keeping a mask, a guard.

What's the point? I've co-operated and I wouldn't have asked for help if I really didn't want it but am left hopeless and unworthy.

23rd September 1997 – Dallinghoo

I'm now back at Mum's. I said goodbye to Tim last Wednesday which was truly saddening and then to Karen, it just hurt so much leaving friends behind.

How am I ever going to break away from all this? If I knew my diet was causing it I could stop the indulgences and eat healthier, anything to eliminate the itching.

All I know is that it is Sunday and I am highly suicidal. Woke up 100% depressed. I can't get rid of those thoughts, death is so tempting at the moment. I hate this, hate the stupidity of it all, of myself. Nothingness. I'm just so tired and low. My guts ache. I'm going to go insane if I don't stop bingeing, my head is getting so twisted and fucked up.

OCTOBER

2nd October 1997 – Felixstowe

I keep making promises I can't stick to. At least I've not binged for 4 days although my consumption of sweets grows every day and the itching is worse. What am I going to do about it?

Also decorating the flat and am trying to think it'll be alright but in the silence thoughts are rife.

All I have now spins around my skull, shut in, shut down and banging about. I can't believe how I lack so much in myself, in confidence, self esteem, belief. Where has it all gone?

I can't live properly or fully. I'm sick of this, fucking sick.

5th October 1997

I've been asked to go into St Clements but I couldn't find a reason not to other than I'm scared to. I can't have any anti depressants in case I OD on them. Out of control and in a state, just deep fucking despair.

And today is Sunday, another day with more desperate thoughts pounding my head. I've a bucket of bricks squashing my brow. Things go backwards every day. I'm shut down and live in my head as everything external is in a spin. I can barely talk for long as there's nothing new, not much to say.

Ian asked me why I'm doing this if I'm not 100% about it . . . it's just something I have to do, regardless of the outcome, if I don't try to live alone. To be honest right now I don't want to be left alone.

I see a foot ahead then I hit a black wall and no space beyond. I've deteriorated so much mentally, physically I hold ground but my head is fucked up and twisting, full of voices that aren't mine, they swamp all other thoughts. I'm so far behind, as bad as I used to be, there's no room for anything good or new inside, it's being blocked. That's why I wish I had the guts to die and release my head from the torment. *Je suis mal à la tete.*

I'm sick in the head.

7th October 1997

I suppose the most difficult thing today has been looking at myself in mirrors, trying on clothes, even just toilet ones. I can't bear to look too long as I'm repulsed, even scared, by what looks back at me.

'Amy Phillips, I love you . . .' I can't truly say it, not today anyway. All I see is a skinny girl, awkward and a mess, tangled hair and glasses. I want to snap my fingers and be well and yet I am so trapped.

15th October 1997

Although I seem to be gaining peace inside and desire a stronger physical form there is discomfort as ever in feeling flesh. I don't understand it. I wish it wouldn't bother me so as it's a constant reminder. Maybe it's purely because I feel very bloated today that's making my presence and unease prominent.

I will not starve and deprive but I must get a sense of structured, good nutrition to feed my brain and body without my reliance on sweets, biscuits and chocolate, it's what I always return to when all else fails.

25th October 1997

Welcome to the world of the girl whose grip was so jaded yesterday that . . . to say on Monday I enter into a nightmare in my desperation to get well. Playford House, slum bungalow. I wish I was off my brain so I didn't know what I'm letting myself in for but sadly in moments of clarity it's chillingly clear. I'm so ill in a restrained way. I hate what this is doing, not only to me but for Mum, to watch her daughter disintegrating, unable to answer for herself. Why should I let them know my plans? I don't want to tell YOU. So much of me wants an end to this but I don't want to die, not in a pointless way, a pressure release to a moment of torment.

The warnings are getting clearer and the time nearer. It's a continual movement with one hell of a lot of relapsing . . . BANG . . . BANG . . . BANG.

Enveloped

Sunday 26th October 1997

I cannot sleep and have been laid here eating biscuit after biscuit and so it goes on until I'm sick inside and sad, sad because I don't want them but the compulsion to cram is rife as I'm restless and uneasy. It's almost like I'm stocking up in case I go hungry! I long for the ability to make myself sick but cannot even try. So tomorrow must be a fresh start regarding diet. The day I am no longer reliant on biscuits and sweets, can it ever happen? Even just one single day would be a triumph. My whole palate needs re-educating, actually my whole body needs feeding properly first, then maybe I would crave and feed on other things instead of basing everything on comfort food; they give me more satisfaction than meals but I lose structure and touch with normal states as my brain is fixated with pleasure boosts and switches off from sense.

Last night was bad, terrible dreams, Susan, Laura and Ian amongst others, set in Leeward Court. My paintings were on the ground and being walked all over, I tried to pick them up. Much to-ing and fro-ing until eventually I ran but it was all slow motion and people kept grabbing me and before I woke they were shouting, 'Don't let go of her, she's ANOREXIC and a danger to herself.'

I was screaming in their faces, desperately trying to struggle free.

Leg pain numbing and intense in sleep, I thought the right shin had been amputated and today the pain is so bad I have felt like passing out as it seeps through the bone. It is empty. Will it crumble and cripple?

DEPRESSION and EATING DISORDER. If only one is treated the other will remain, if I am never to be free then . . . I know maybe the depression can only ever be managed to a liveable, tolerable degree but the eating disorder must be eradicated otherwise it will be a constant torment and nothing will have changed. I am ready to fight, you fucking bastard. I am scared because I hear you getting stronger, your voice more cutting, critical, you'd rather keep me in chaos, fearing fat, fearing flesh and it isn't me. I know it isn't me.

Monday 27th October 1997 – Playford House,
St Clement's Hospital

The battle is on. Since I walked into Playford my body has shut down. Made the decision not to eat or drink, even speaking is hard. Just don't want to let anything pass my lips, yet I'm hungry and I'm cold, combining torment. I have to eat something but . . . fucking hell. The old anorexic sadness is back. Last food was 10 a.m. declined dinner and it is now 4.30 p.m. so six and a half hours.

I hate this and so intensely hate myself.

Also been thinking a lot about making myself sick, actually striving and practising until it comes easily. If I succeed though I'm losing further, adding another complexity. Do I, don't I, DO I, DON'T I? Every hour is fucking torment and tears. Shuffled steps, limbs weighted, each movement too much effort. This low, so low I lie on the floor for comfort. Scared by the surroundings. Sleep. Sedation equals security but I have neither so am truly aware I don't want to be here. Same old questions answered and asked. I should have it tattooed to avoid this tedious repetition.

Is this a bridging gap to a clinic?

Went for tea and it was a crappy puddle of mince and a sad salad thus I promptly walked away from it and laid back on the floor. Mum and Mike came, both proceeded to get annoyed at my lack of will to get better and eat. I wanted them to fuck right off and leave me, never come back. How the hell would they feel if they'd arrived here, completely alien environment, and basically just left with no idea of what is what. They haven't a clue so shouldn't make assumptions. I'm tired, tearful and irrational, the last thing I fucking want is proper food brought into me.

Have broken my pact and had something (10 hours). I can't taste anything so . . .

Once I've adjusted it'll be ok. I'm not going to put on a mask for others anymore. Give me the drugs and get on with it, it's just the junked up limbo I dread.

NOTES ON SELF ESTEEM

Treating yourself well is part of self esteem so I must stop the self punishment and become aware of myself, my body and learn to listen to it. My biggest enemy is SELF DOUBT. Achievement comes through believing and valuing yourself. You choose your own thoughts so previously held attitudes, old habits and behaviours must be let go of. I'm unhelpful to myself by compulsive stuffing to hide feelings, bingeing when I panic and focusing on sweet treats, craved and comfort foods.

A combination of fear and thoughts about feelings being unimportant leads to a build up of anxiety and worry causing exhaustion.

3 ways life would be different if I believed in myself: I'd be stronger, more capable, alive.
3 new goals: to accept myself, to accept others wanting to accept me and just believe I can be.
3 new ways I'd choose to act: freely, without anxiety obsessions or safety nets tangling my thoughts.

Thursday 30th October 1997

This place is soul destroying, I lie here dead, dead inside and sleeping. Headbanging and groggy. My eating so very structured, no chaos now but not enough food is going in as most ends up in the bin. No taste, no pleasure. Toast is the safety net. My appetite gone, no urge any more. I feel worse than ever because I'm so numb. Being here keeps me safe from change because I'm not confronting anything; the longer it remains the harder it'll be if I ever get into a clinic since my resistance will have built up further. This evening I'm so empty and alone.

A) WHAT AM I? Strong, intelligent, creative but also have the potential to be loving, sexual, glowing, attractive, sharing but instead I'm hiding!
B) I want to achieve good physical and mental health, happiness, freedom and inner peace. In order to do this I must start feeding, nurturing and listening to my body. PLEASE.
C) I need to let go of my eating disorder since it is keeping me trapped in suspended animation.
I stand the other side of the gate, it's like I've a bunch of keys in my hand but can't find the one to open the lock. Essentially I have the basic tools for recovery but they are clanking about inside me. I keep trying different keys but have yet to find the right one.
D) HELPFUL THOUGHTS
I can get better, there is life without torment ahead if I am truly prepared to shake this thing.
I am worth it as I have the potential to be astounding!

NOVEMBER
Saturday 1st November 1997
I'm out of hospital until Monday morning and I realise I'm as depressed outside but in a different way.

Whem I'm IN it is because I'm frustrated, just sleeping and feeling so bloody numb. When I'm OUT it is because of reality, of my inadequacies and distance. Aaargh.

Enveloped

Monday 3rd November 1997

It has been one hell of a morning. I went back to Playford for 10 a.m. and just started crying, walking back to the ward. New woman next to me snoring like a pig. I laid there and cried and cried. Tense, panicky and wound up. After OT I knew I had to get out of there, all I could think about was grabbing my bag and running off. Eventually rang Mum, she dashed up, tried to convince me I'd jeopardise getting into a clinic but I couldn't honestly promise to stay put. Another 24 hours in that place, it's like being trapped in a very slow nightmare, the moments grinding away.

I fucking binged last night because I didn't want to go but I was trying to pretend, be brave about it. I've been overwhelmed by such consuming pure hatred.

The weekend was good, enjoyable, stayed with Mum on Saturday and saw H on Sunday, the only blip being the binge. Everything is chaos, chaotic inside and confusing. Emotional, physical, food. I have to focus on looking forward and finding a release from all this.

So that is where the story should end
yet I've come full circle again.

Wednesday 5th November 1997 – Felixstowe

I need to create a new philosophy to live my life by, to encompass all areas and allow them to become real, visible and most of all comfortable.

I DENY my body, its physical form I keep stunted.

I CREATE CHAOS with eating, through cravings, bingeing. I lose the voice of reason and live on the impulse. I create chaos with alcohol which often fuels a binge further, to blur my days, to feel warm inside and a little. I create chaos with ingrained behaviour and patterns that I always return to. As if I don't already have enough pain I cause more torment through the above.

I NEED TO ACCEPT panic when it sweeps through me and confront it. Physical discomfort, confusion and uncertainty as all of these cause me to cram and fill myself as a way of distracting.

ALL THIS AND . . .

I think I feel better today. This evening I managed a vaguely proper meal and have eaten at regular intervals throughout the day. It's a start. My expectations are far beyond the reality as the resistance has more power than I give it credit for. I just need to slowly undermine it, subtly instead of kicking it head on as I hurt myself with constant batterings. Think of it as effervescent, slowly dissolving, eroding and dispersing, twisting and turning until it has crumbled and sunk. It may leave a bitter taste on the tongue but once it's gone the relief will come.

Thursday 6th November 1997

Being in these kinds of places makes you more tolerant, you see people in such states and how they change daily and you learn not to judge, as it is illness that causes the behaviour. You often aren't even aware that you are acting out of place. One thing I did notice being in Playford was that I seemed to almost take on the persona of a mental illness. Your whole body language changed in that atmosphere and made depression worse.

Saturday 8th November 1997

Last night a lot of thoughts were swimming about and yearnings. I kept thinking about Tim and aching for him yet also wanting to throw my arms around Ian and say how much I love him, not that that would change anything. I'm torn between two people, neither of which have any future in a relationship sense. Basically I'm involved in two immensely strong friendships. The power of emotion, of feeling, can be frightening if you don't know what to do with it. By the time I'd got to bed I lay awake and was craving, craving physical, sexual contact, I was a buzz with the need for it. How it used to feel . . .

Sunday 9th November 1997

Today is exhaustion and oddness inside, a sense of feeling strangely ill but unidentifiably so. The weather is shit, all overcast and rain and I am thinking, what if I am too scared to ever step out into the world? What is the point of it all then?

Wednesday 12th November 1997

Since seeing Mary a lot of thoughts about this clinic have been running through my mind. It has to be done but I'm scared, scared of remaining as I am, scared of what lies ahead.

Will they understand I can't eat bread or dairy products? Will I be made to eat margarine? Will they believe me?

I'm suspicious, weary. Are they going to trick me? There are no other options though because this time I cannot climb back alone. I can't beat it purely under my own steam. The will is there but I'm stuck, stuck at this point.

Talking to Mary I realise it's not the weight that makes you eligible for treatment, it's more to do with behaviour, attitudes, so I needn't lose weight to prove a point, I don't know if I could anyway.

I'm in a holding place, existing and numb.

Thursday 13th November 1997

Panic pending.

Enveloped

Sunday 16th November 1997

Panic has become unease and it's smothering me. I can't lose it even in sleep but then I lie awake until the early hours fretting, thinking and wanting, just wanting answers and to be away from all this. Tomorrow I will know.

This weekend I've felt lost and tormented but in a peaceful way. The tablets have reduced the chaos to calm but the problem still lies inside, very much alive.

Three hours of pure absorption in *Schindlers List*, stunning. I am struck by the beauty of Liam Neeson, black and white, bold and striking. I've also read about healing, the spiritual form, and it brings into question thoughts. Have I been disconnected from the physical form by trying to live in spirit rather than reality? I've shunned, denied my body, becoming skin and bone, stunting physical growth when I should have believed in myself, in my presence and in living.

Instead I've blocked out reminders of my body, so harshly and with such hate. Anorexia and its hold, the behaviour, its power, it has the control, not you, it's devious and underhand. I've been climbing walls to get away from it but now ahead lies a dead end so dark and dense, I've weakened and it's laughing at me.

Oh fuck, fucking fuck, even my anger just melts into despair, alone it will live inside of me and I can't face that any more. I have got to get help soon because the chaos is coming and that means it will have won.

Tuesday 18th November 1997

Finally we're getting somewhere, saw Dr G yesterday and he's prepared to give me funding for a clinic, thank God. I was so relieved I just cried when we got out of there. Relief is immense, now I'm scared but excited scared. I have to choose where, is it to be Dukes Priory in Chelmsford, St Georges or

143

The Maudlsey. Apparently I have this choice because the London ones tackle more complex cases but do I want to be cut off? London fills me with a sense of glamour and grimness I adore but it'll be difficult to be visited; the units are part of big psychiatric hospitals and I won't really see London as I'm there in hospital. I see Chelmsford tomorrow and if it looks OK then that will be fine. I don't want to waste time, or any more time than is necessary. All I can hope is to have a place by Christmas, even if I only get an admission date, at least it'll be set. This is my last attempt. If this doesn't ground me I'm fucked. But it will . . . I have to believe I have the strength to live in a physical form and to re-invent myself, become the person I was too scared to allow.

I feel like weeping for what I'm losing, weeping because of uncertainty and partly for the thought of being free. The next few months, despite all I have been through, will be the hardest; it'll be enforced separation as I decide what's me and what's not me. I'm shrouded in sickness, even the merest glimpse of a possible me is quickly covered in confusion and pushed back into black.

Thursday 20th November 1997

FUCK. It's all going too fast. I saw Dukes Priory yesterday, rang Dr G's secretary, then I spoke to Mum and the funding will be ready 9.30 a.m. tomorrow and in I go. I'm not ready, which sounds stupid; it's just I thought it would take a couple of days or so, leaving me enough time to tie up loose ends and sort the bits to take with me and basically make the most of my last few days in the outside world.

Now I'm anxious as hell. Nothing's sorted because I can't pack tonight as there is no electricity in the flat. Aaaargh. I feel tense, tired and sick.

What am I going to do? Mind's racing.

Enveloped

Friday 21st November 1997 – Dukes Priory Hospital,
Chelmsford
Well, against all conflicting odds I am here in Dukes Priory, came in at 3 p.m. It has just gone 9 p.m. and I'm feeling quite relaxed and positive. It's the start of everything.

Earlier I felt such a deep sense of loss, not unlike bereavement, very bewildering, but I guess it's because I'm in the process of separation. I've identified the anorexia, we're both aware of that, it has repulsed, created despair, I've looked at it with contempt and this is the ultimate act of FUCK YOU to it. In order to go through this, in order to cope with increased meal plans etc. I have to shut off a part of me and get on with the job in hand, after all that is why I'm here.

Your days are numbered and you know it.

Sunday 23rd November 1997
It's strange, I'm so calm, detached even passive, there is an odd inner peace. It's like I've grown out of my anorexia. I'm not saying it has gone but it's that I've separated us and I'm beginning now the process of physically restoring the damage it's done and getting the old associated image replaced. I know it's not going to be getting any easier, physically it will hurt and that is my worst area: physical pain and discomfort are hard to bear. My guts are ballooning and gassing, even with nowt on it's like I've a band around my belly restricting it. 2 days and it seems longer.

It'll be good when I'm allowed to choose my menu and make informed choices because I'm so far removed from any active interest in what I eat that it needs re-educating. Also when they trust me. I hate not being trusted as I offer up my honesty; it's all I have and to be doubted does knock the remaining drop of self esteem that is present.

Enveloped

Monday 24th November 1997

From this afternoon's group discussion qualities I've realised would be good to possess are independence, freedom, appreciation, aspirations . . . unrestricted . . . all coupled with inner strength, endurance and honesty I already own to create a healthy whole. Anorexia has owned me and become an identity, destroying what I'd developed and wasn't secure enough in and as time went by I became scared to identify, admit and acknowledge. A crux has very much been this crisis of identity, the lack of self image, the ultimate in self denial. It is a deep fear, acceptance.

Tuesday 25th November 1997

I've come back from dinner and I sat there thinking what the hell am I doing here? Well, the answer is obviously to regain my body and accept and own it but these people are Aaaargh! It is absolutely doing my head in, they pick, dissect, play about with the food, take forever to eat it. Such anorexic behaviour makes me realise I am nothing like that. It's odd, because since I've come in here my eating disorder has ceased to be the mammoth, soul destroying beast that racked me. At the moment I see clearly, aware that I will recover but that depression could still be a remaining element.

I'm so calm, clear and aware, it is a freeing sensation. I am free to be me.

The tedium of laborious rules, being treated almost childlike, having to ask if I can use my loo. No wonder I can't relax and have a good crap because I don't want to spend too long in there in case they get suspicious. It makes me angry and frustrated with it all really. Everyone's so tamed.

Also on eating plan 2 from tomorrow so that's splendid, reckon I can cope, yeah.

Get up, get on and get out.

Enveloped

Wednesday 26th November 1997

Last night was odd, basically after 9 p.m. snack (Maltesers) I started to suddenly burn up and felt very flushed, major headbanging, dizzy, nausea, windy, vision disintegrating and really felt like I would black out. Truly horrible but it happened again after lunch while I was still at the table. Could be a viral thingy, they think, or a possible link being chocolate as I had chocolate sponge for afters. Who knows? The dietician has said to leave off it for now. Crazy, I used to experience this loads but figured it was my constant sugar and chocolate bombardment that caused it; maybe now I'll get this mess sorted out once and for all. Anyway, despite all that, it's been fine today. Yeah.

Rash still rife and also got a lovely card off Mum.

Thursday 27th November 1997

Well today has held a lot, but first I must write down bits of my dreams from last night. Part of it took place in an old psychiatric hospital. I was walking down a lamp lit road, the tarmac was shiny and wet, I think it was still raining. Just as I went up to the door several doctors and nurses were getting into their cars and waved and spoke to me. I remember the door seemed enormous and daunting. Inside I was greeted by Mark, there were the girls off this ward and a few other familiar places. Mark was chatting as ever, very quickly. I looked up into the high ceiling, there were loads of banisters and a staircase which seemed to link but in fact there was only one right way as the others just took you off into other rooms e.g. a refrigeration store with racks of raw meat, a kitchen, a shoe display . . . I was running around the place, bumping into obstacles. In a downstairs room were a couple of armchairs and a pool table. I got comfy in a chair and my Dad came in and we gave each other a massive cuddle then we started playing pool while chatting.

Another part I was with another girl in a consultant's room,

HOW DO I LOOK?

Name: *AMY PHILLIPS* Date: *27th November 1997* Week No: *1*

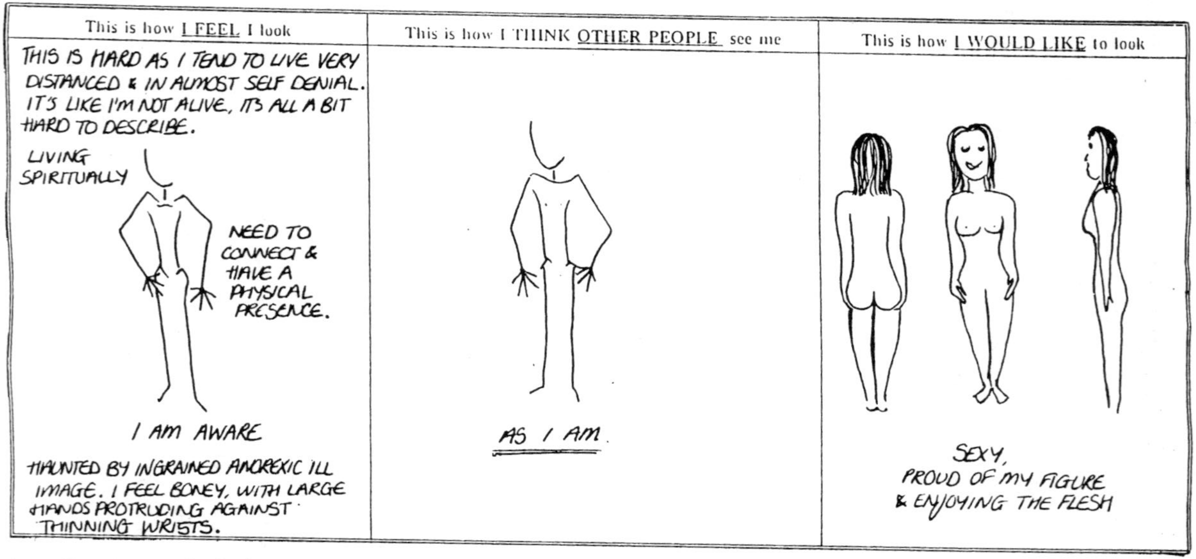

This is how I FEEL I look	This is how I THINK OTHER PEOPLE see me	This is how I WOULD LIKE to look
THIS IS HARD AS I TEND TO LIVE VERY DISTANCED & IN ALMOST SELF DENIAL. IT'S LIKE I'M NOT ALIVE, IT'S ALL A BIT HARD TO DESCRIBE.		
LIVING SPIRITUALLY		
NEED TO CONNECT & HAVE A PHYSICAL PRESENCE.		
I AM AWARE	AS I AM.	SEXY, PROUD OF MY FIGURE & ENJOYING THE FLESH
HAUNTED BY INGRAINED ANOREXIC ILL IMAGE. I FEEL BONEY, WITH LARGE HANDS PROTRUDING AGAINST THINNING WRISTS.		

- Draw this every Sunday between evening meal and going to bed.
- Discuss it with your therapist on Monday.
- Discussed with: ______________________ On: ______________________

he turned to her and said, 'You're not pregnant,' but pointing at me, said, 'You are!' So last night was very disturbed, kept waking, chest pain.

Friday 28th November 1997

Didn't finish yesterday's entry as I went to do some yoga and relaxation which was rather good but I'm not very strong, bit of a shock to the system, movement! The relaxation was well . . . ends up being a bizarre experience. It seems as I'm forced to connect with the body, become aware, tears start coming and it's like I feel years of pain inside and tension in the muscles increases It is a painful experience. With my eyes closed the pyramid and third eye return, floating in monochrome transparency. This often happens when I receive healing or attempt deep relaxation. Also lots of blinding light like staring at the sun.

What else happened yesterday? Spent a good few hours in Broomfield A & E, been told my rash is definitely an allergic reaction.

Saturday 29th November 1997

It all just hurts . . . it's 11.40 p.m. I'm tired, can't sleep so have had to give into another sleeper. My guts are churning, feeling uncomfortable and bloaty, the smell being released is ugh, very rotten indeed and pretty much going for it tonight. Belching a lot but it's not easing the feeling though. Hot, flushing and whites of eyes have turned pinky too. This is just an account of the physical things for now, there is more interesting stuff later but I must really rest.

Basically the rash was clearing up as I'm on a dairy free menu (or as close as possible!) but at about 8 p.m. I started feeling odd inside, kind of shaky like you're going to pass out, achy and the rash on the left shin has got a lot worse, from being red and angry it has developed further with discoloured patches. It is getting silly . . . I feel shit but there's nowt to ease it all at this precise moment and once again I'm surrounded by that rotten old stench . . .

DECEMBER
Tuesday 2nd December 1997

I am sick of listening to people going on and on about food, it is doing my fucking head in, it's either decisions, excuses, dislikes, comments, questioning what it tastes like, how it looks and the list goes on. My gut is bloated and irritating after lunch so would you just shut up.

The evening was thrown into turmoil by ward round, it got a bit intense, so much more than with Dr G and caught me off guard with the questioning. I felt like I was sat there trying to justify my anorexia, the disconnecting, but there are so many contributing factors that all I could suggest was one, then I totally disintegrated into tears saying I was sick of being ill. So now I'm confused. I thought positivity was me but maybe it's not, it's just a different form of detachment to help me deal with being here, kidding myself I've worked through things. Basically it has caused immense self doubt in my current portrayals of strength: it has served to undermine.

Thursday 4th December 1997

Bloody hell, I'm trying to sleep without a sleeper yet vividly returning are images of the art installation I created in May 1993. It just fucking summed up everything, it was like a final bit of creative genius before nose diving into anorexia completely. I keep seeing the skeleton I placed under a muslin sheet with the body shape and death mask and feet. The inward spiralling path, the bubbling frustration, the lowered ceiling, coloured light through windows, the whole bloody claustrophobic, autobiographical creation that took five weeks of pure dedication and drained me. In a way it said, this is my experience. I knew at that stage I could never achieve any more than that room and the skeleton corner was me: subconsciously I knew something was wrong, even at the time some part of me knew. I guess at that point I'd got too tired and vulnerable to notice and the summer sank into sadness.

Friday 5th December 1997

Jeez, talk about suspicious, Dr F (or whatever his name is) thinks I'm too enthusiastic!!! That it's a cover so I'm not facing my feelings. I admit the positivity is a real kind of transformation but it's not the false sense of trying to kid myself it'll be OK, it's a culmination of knowing this time all the help being offered is for the duration and I've an immense inner strength and relief beaming through. Of course I realise this is an easy patch, a time of relief and relative safety. I am detached from my feelings to a certain degree but there needs to be some space. I do think, I do feel pain although it often comes in the night, in dreams, when I'm looking for sleep that only a tablet can achieve. The shit will come, there will be panic, friction, agitation, irritation and questioning, as long as I keep questioning.

Sunday 7th December 1997

Feeling shite and nauseous . . . interrupted there by lunch but am now allowed to spend supervision time in my room, it's to give me space and perhaps allow more clarity in thoughts. I'm finding it very hard to be around eating disorders 24 hours a day, I guess because I was so plagued by it so consistently that I am now looking for some sense of normality, not only in environment, in attitudes, in behaviour, in words, in conversation. It's not that by wanting this I'm blanking I have a problem, it's more that I feel so much further on, that I'm progressing to the surface. For others they have come from family straight into here so already have a sense of sharing mealtimes normally before their illness and will once again return to it; but for me, our family rarely ate together, we all did our own thing so the normality I crave is important as it was not ingrained before.

If behaviour gets bizarre, alone you don't see it, there's no gauge by which to keep it real. See, I need to engrave patterns, see realistic behaviour, do things I feel are healthy, breathe the air, see sunlight, even just walking to the paper shop.

Even in my room I'm not away from the others twining about food and it's tedious, it's negative. I'm using everything to shut them off, shut it out but it's blacking out all thoughts. The things that are trying to come forward are lost in black. So days are spent lethargic and shutdown until I shut my door at night in search of sleep and instead memories, recognition, feelings are rife when all I want is rest. This is what needs to be turned around so instead of culminating in nightmares and horror, I can remember and work at it.

The sense of negativity within the unit has lead to thoughts of discharging myself. I know it's not a scared or running thought, reaction; it's come from the tedium and repetition that I am trying to rise above, but it is using so much inner energy and draining the resources I need in order to focus on me progressing because that's a damn sight more important.

I want more distance from the group.

. . . this evening I'm not even sure I want to be alive any more, not like this, not in this discomfort. The itchy, scratching inside is back and the bloating since mid afternoon snack. Oh I don't know, something is still agitating the bowels, of course IBS is stress related but I can feel it in different ways. I've lived with IBS, to see and know what's what and you can't describe the sensation to someone who's not experienced the almost mind bending agony it can cause. Also note I am going to go crazy, I have to hang in there until Tuesday and see Chris, rice cakes AAAAARGH! And that vegan ice cream just repeats and repeats and repeats, it's grim.

So I've sat full of sickness and sadness thinking if I can survive the next 10 weeks, get through to the other side . . . Is the depression back? I didn't think I wanted to die anymore. I don't know, it would be a short, sharp end to it this time. When I was in the depths of anorexia, I had no power, no control. I felt helpless and trapped but now I have power, I know I won't starve once I'm secure in a clear plan regarding foods etc, I'm more scared of compulsive behaviour. I'm totally confused, I think myself into circles. I don't feel anorexic any longer but how will I ever know, especially in here?

Monday 8th December 1997

It's Monday not Tuesday but I lose track, it doesn't make much difference either way. Note: oats re-emerging undigested. The low is so deep, the physical pain, fullness, causing discomfort leading to discomfort in my skin and from this comes not wanting to be in myself because then I don't have the pain . . . but that's not how it really works.

Quite suicidal but without the strength, the only way I'd go here is to run straight through my fucking window. Today I miss T incredibly. I wish I could see him, he has been in my thoughts along with wanting contact with other friends whom I'd normally phone to keep in touch, even write, but I can't face writing, explaining again and again where I am.

Sense of going backwards.

Tuesday 9th December 1997

Sleep troubled, mood very low. I sat at the breakfast table staring off into the world outside, forlornly focusing on the almost silver bare limbed branches, longing to touch that tree, to feel something solid, something real.

Isn't it amazing how mood changes? It's been dire until I got my 10 minutes of air and then saw Chris. It is nearly 11.30 p.m. and I feel good, a lot mentally lighter and bouncy. Have just swapped some trousers. They are the first thing I've worn for ages that I feel good in. This is what I need to do, start wearing clothes that I am comfortable in, not slobby, hiding away but instead feel vaguely sexy so I can see the potential, look in that mirror and approve of Amy Phillips and her physical presence. I've also formed these little blueberry breasts (first description that popped into my head). All good stuff but I must rest, sleep and preserve my energy, she's away with the Verve.

Wednesday 10th December 1997

9.30 a.m. and I've been for four shits already! What is this becoming, the diary of a woman recording her stool formation! It is important though.

Still feeling good this morning, could have wished for more peaceful sleep but unfortunately not so. Am quite tired and today is full of groups. Have also started on more anti-depressants.

Thursday 11th December 1997

Well yesterday was splendid (to a point), felt very bouncy, mentally lighter, positive and quite chilled out. After morning shits stomach and gut settled, pain free all day and that felt damn good. Chris brought in various things for me to try out and as of today I'm on a 5 day exclusion diet.

Come 10 p.m. last night I had what felt like stitch, got very bloated and my insides were twisting, very painful; slept very badly as I couldn't get comfortable.

Today I've felt like I've been run over by a steamroller, pale and drained. Stitch pain is still nagging and nagging away so finally decided to see a doctor and I have a possible kidney and urinary infection. I keep mislaying pens today. Where was I? Right, so 1 day in 3 weeks I actually felt relieved of discomfort and pain, it's a start at least.

Basically have spent today mainly in bed, too exhausted to do anything so I've let myself be, to rest. Sometimes I feel people might think me a hypochondriac but I'm not. For too long I've been turned away and I've kept these physical things enclosed because no one took them seriously and when you've been labelled as ANOREXIC you've no hope as it is all put back to that. Who's going to trust an anorexic anyway, let alone give credence to their thoughts especially if it's regarding foods, allergies etc., but I'm here now and it may take more than 3 months to sort the physical side out and regain a level of health.

Friday 12th December 1997

Most of today has been spent lethargically in bed, trying to rest. I get so tired, it's a real effort even to be up all day at the moment, I just find it hard . . . Gut pains are minimal although this evening there has been some bloating and wind. Ah well, of course I don't expect them to suddenly improve. I realise it is going to take time for them to settle. Just need sleep.

Monday 15th December 1997

The past few days I have been in bed feeling very tired, drained and achy plus a fucking serious migraine situation on Sunday. Although today started off pretty much in the same vein, it has improved greatly. Have made the effort to dress properly and that felt good, but once again this evening my intense internal aches and stitch-like sensation returned as it has done of late, with the left side suffering worse. It's like I've been repeatedly kicked in the kidneys and it is so tender I cannot get comfortable.

The positive things are that I'm calm with a sense of inner

peace and everyday I become more real in myself. I have a stronger self belief with a feeling of security, secure in knowing what is me and liking it. I'm enjoying, enjoying the release from inner turmoil, confusion, despair and hatred. It feels very good to be free of internal battles and deep emotional anguish. Nothing seems to be troubling me (apart from physical pain). It's all so strange. I have noticed I'm swearing shit loads and that I stand up for my rights and will challenge. I don't feel exactly angry, more frustrated and annoyed hence I say things bluntly and often feel very aggressive with it. Mmmm.

Friday 19th December 1997

Well, this week has gone and have spent most of the days exhausted, drained and with physical pain in the bones, in the muscles, especially the shin. Some old pains that have been there for many years. I just can't believe how fucking knackered I am, more so than others, it just hits me – WHAM. One and a half good days out of seven if I'm lucky as the rest of the time I'm absolutely fucked.

It is hard to explain my immense tiredness. I'm not lazy (as that's often been said). I've felt like this since I was 14 but been told it's growing pains, it's period pains, it's because of your anorexia, living at a low body weight, excuses, excuses, yet even last April at a proper weight I still felt so fucking ill and in pain, some days I could barely move so had to lie on my front in bed. It's frustrating as I'd like to be able to do more but physically I can't, it's got nothing to do with emotional things as my head is clear, my thinking has improved remarkably, I'm more aware, more real.

My, my, I seem to have been a mass of dodgy health for far too long. Can I face the rest of life being so damn done in? I'm just clinging to the thought that life will get easier, eventually!

Also Ian came over to see me which was lovely.

I've been searching for any emotional conflicts or turmoil but so far have not found any, to be quite honest. So many others are full of it and it's almost expected from me otherwise I'm not in touch, or denying my problems, but I'm not going to create any just for the sake of it. Maybe it's them needing a psychological link in order to explain away what I'm experiencing physically.

I've spent so many years fucked up and confused by the shite in my head that I've worked it over again and again until I've been able to turn around the unproductive and negative thoughts. Little by little it comes together in gradual steps to enable you to actively resolve the perceived problems and areas of conflict until it suddenly hits you just how you'd managed to move on and accept the unchangeable past.

BOXING DAY

I can't even begin to describe how desperate I am . . . not in a suicidal fashion, just despair at not being able to eat the things I want, crave. I'm sitting waiting for another bland dinner to come up yet my mind races through the foods I could have if only my body would let me. If only: that pretty much sums up the scenario. Really my diet needs broadening as soon as possible. SERIOUSLY. I crave, I fantasize yet I know the consequences. Damn you, Amy Phillips, for being strong.

Since we last spoke, well I've been once more ill, flat in bed and suffering, more tablets than a pharmacy down my throat and everything hurts. My face also spasmed horrendously last night (a reaction to Maxalon) and I ended up with a needle in my bum!

It's been me and Bec here since 2.30 p.m. Christmas Eve.

I have spent most of this week in a toxic haze in nightmares and dreams beginning, ending and surrounding Playford which have left me disturbed.

27th December 1997

Have slept poorly and am now wide awake and feeling strange inside, an almost chilling sensation, an uneasiness of warmth and aching almost equatable to period pains.

6.19 a.m. and the banging downstairs has begun again. I can't work out whether they're throwing themselves repeatedly against something or just slamming down and down and down.

6.23 a.m. and once more I wish for sleep . . .

Things are getting harder, I'm struggling so badly. If I could wish for one thing it would be to curl up in someone's warm, loving arms and sleep, but instead I'm in Dukes, alone in bed, my only comfort being a water bottle and it sucks, this whole situation sucks. I'm tired, tearful, in pain and fed up.

This is all just a vicious circle. I'm sick of eating bland shite, meals are a chore, my infection and pains are rife adding to feeling rank, want to find out what I can have and SOON, want to leave and be well but without going through the physical trial and error.

Have also started refusing the anti-depressants, wise choice or not? It's been given so erratically this past week that it really isn't doing much anyway. If my mood lowers it comes from physical shitness that I can't handle.

Tablets, tablets, tablets they just keep on coming . . .

28th December 1997

Today I've been bad, in a bad way, anxious, tearful, nauseous and fed up. I've been crying because my guts are so badly upset. Thankfully Mum came earlier and it's been good to see her, she's cheered me up no end, just talking, having a cuddle. I get so lonely sometimes and distanced in here. Will I ever see the real world again? Of course, but it's getting there. Ideally I'd like to be eating a normal diet and getting the extra in . . . even intravenously which seems drastic but I am desperate. It's been questioned that possibly wanting that is anorexic. NO is my answer. I have proved to myself that I'm not, when I came in I knew that if anorexia was lingering, then as I gained ground that is when problems would begin, but I can quite honestly say that I'm comfortable in my emerging body: it's surprised me and I'm pleased.

It's 4.59 p.m. and I'm feeling more positive than earlier, it's just when you're stuck in shitness it makes me realise how much agony and discomfort I've lived in and it scares and shakes me.

29th December 1997

Have been thinking a lot about this year, it's been a busy, chaotic one that's been full of experience and changes. Emotionally I've begun to feel, I've felt love, the warmth, the excitement it brings and to touch, accept being touched. It's still in the early stages but this year has helped show what's me and what isn't, through chasing dreams, instability, Keswick, psychiatric wards, fear, Tim, insecurity and illness. This all needs deeper thought given to it in daylight and reams.

Tonight I am angry though, angry at being sore inside and this place. Still in catch 22 so have had a bath, listened to the Verve and feel like ripping down these walls. It's an indescribable strength which is striving me to pull up a hard mask and disguise the intensity of pain, form myself and concentrate my energies to start looking, looking at what is needed to get out. PATIENCE and peace of mind plus the ability to blank out snipes as they concentrate on others rather than look at the stupidity of their own actions and gripes. I shall move further down the ward for sanctuary too. At least in bed it washes over me. Their immaturity and indulgence in illness is what pushes vicious tongues but if they wanted us to be equal I'd gladly share my physical shitness for the chance to eat freely without allergies. At least I am secure in myself (in here) and will stand my ground as this is a big FUCK YOU to all that has held me down.

Enveloped

Enveloped

1998

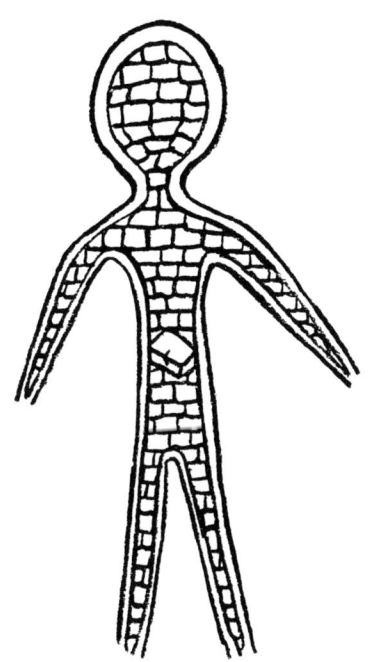

JANUARY

Right, bastards, it's the 2nd January 1998. I didn't bother to see the New Year in, too tired and it's always a let down especially in here! So what's new? Lots of toxic dreams and am exhausted by coping with pain. Last night there was a tunnel made of video screens showing continual images; I'd walked through it and noticed one had a shark slamming into it which freaked me slightly so I tried to ignore it and ran through. All the screens went blank, it was silent and dark. I waited . . . then all at once they fused back into life but I found myself surrounded by the shark again, on every screen, above, below, the sides, ahead. Frozen I stood, eyes tightly shut, hands over my ears to block out the ear splitting sound. At which point I jerked awake.

Have seen Dr G today and that man confuses me at times. I gain weight and assume he will be pleased that I'm back onto making progress but instead I'm left thinking I'm not addressing things by being ill! Well excuse me. Also he thinks I do have an eating disorder as it can't be a mere case of food intolerances causing it, mmm. I beg to disagree and we shall see in due course.

6th January 1998

I'm on top form, my weight is going on a treat (now 7st 6lbs); a stone to go then I'm GOING! Yes I can do this within the next six weeks. At this rate my periods will be back in the next few months. It's all distributing nicely too, I've been taking a good look at myself in the mirror and I'm excited, I like what I see. Entering into uncharted territory with a sane head. Although physically I've been here before I was still in chaos, fucked up, ill and bingeing.

Wednesday 7th January 1998

Today I've been full of sadness and tears. Last night I had a very strange dream, can't remember exactly what it involved but I know Dad was in it. Spoke to Mum and ended up in tears and I've been thinking a lot about Ian too. I'm just really missing being able to talk and see friends, I'm so cut off in here. Empty and lonely, no physical contact when sometimes all I want is a hug from somebody I love. Also been thinking about T. Basically I'm missing everyone I've known.

I'm dead set on getting out in five weeks, it's all my thoughts drift back to, that's why I can't sleep at night. It's planning, it's dreams and desires. I've also thought about old times . . .

SPEAK YOUR OWN TRUTH

Enveloped

Thursday 8th January 1998

The problem is you can live too much in the past or wish too much for the future, either way you're neglecting the here and now. Life passes by and you're too busy living in dreams to counteract the discomfort of the moment; by that I mean for example my time in here, each day I wish away, each week can't be over quick enough as I count each pound as a sign of getting nearer. If I'm not careful I will have left without using what's here, as I neglect the group, the other girls, in exchange for my own company, it isn't a bad thing to actually want and experience being with myself, watching television, writing letters, thinking or just resting, but as ever there is always a BUT . . . I need a balance. Although it's strange living with a bunch of lost and tormented souls. Charley is between the two, at least she wants to get better.

This morning I was woken by screaming.

Strange toxic dreams, again, and in parts quite sensual.

Also thoughts, thoughts about the energy I once held and will return, the sexual energy so strongly a part of me fused into creativity directed my whole being. This leads me to how to cope with it. Last time it returned I was uneasy, uneasy as I had no real outlet, uneasy because I wanted. I shut down because it was too uncomfortable to be so driven with desire, so full of this energy that had nowhere to go, as though I might explode through frustration. So why do I have such a problem with my sexuality? Which is essentially where it all lies. But what is it, sexuality? Certainly it's very physical, very creative, it's the experience of being alive in our body. Maybe that's what scares me, the intensity of my own sexuality especially if I don't know how the hell to express it, safely. It doesn't scare me consciously as I know how it feels to be truly scared. I always thought my biggest fear would be finding me and living in a body I couldn't cope with. I honestly believed that as I gained more weight that

I'd be fearing the flesh, being uncomfortable in my skin, but I'm not and I don't know why. Not that I wish for turmoil such as that but maybe it's that old anorexic label sunk in again, that is what should happen but it hasn't.

It's been strange being depressed from such a young age. It leaves you scared, you feel as though you're mental, deranged, distant. It never seemed so until I became a teenager then the difference became so marked, I felt so cruel inside, so cold and cut off as I viewed the world through my own detached lens, created and compounded from years of teasing, years of intense emotional pain, turmoil and seeing things hurt people, people I loved, and knowing I could do nothing to change any of it. When you have no self esteem, a sense of self doesn't matter, and when you feel that damaged and sick in the head nothing makes sense anymore, it all crowds in and becomes too much to take. Daily batterings, vicious words, recurring thoughts, you're just hitting the wall and it bounces back at you and in it goes again and again until you've seen and heard it all before but it won't let up, won't let you rest: tortured dreams reinforcing, creating another layer, it just keeps on stacking up, pushing you further down because you don't understand why it's all happening. The only feeling is that you're warped and insane. Your reality has changed.

Tonight I feel like eating and eating, as though I have an endless hunger, a comfort eat. This is one thing I need to be very careful of in my urgency to gain weight that I don't push it too far and slip into old habits . . .

Saturday 10th January 1998

Saw Dr G, and as for wanting to be given more leeway and freedom, that's all up the shitter. I have no life and it's fucking me off as I'm restless and want to start getting on and out of this vegetative state. Came out and just cried, cried because I'm so fucking frustrated with it. Seems like the only thing to do is eat my way out of the Priory. That's all there is and right now all I wish for is bed and deep sleep to help me forget but it's way too early for Nytol and still a snack to go.

SEEK COMFORT FROM SLEEP

Sunday 11th January 1998

Short of confining myself to bed 24 hours a day and having even less of a life . . . Man it's frustrating. Everything I do uses energy, thinking, typing, writing, moving, stressing! I've already begun to increase input anyway. I know I can only do all I can, so should ease up on myself really because worrying about it won't help me in anyway whatsoever. Each hold up is delaying me, adding more weeks, more confinement when I need to have some sort of activity. So my head is in a spin.

Will my body decide when it's had enough?

Monday 12th January 1998

Slept very badly, only 2 broken hours. At one point I had to keep the light on because I was so freaked out by my first dream that I didn't want to fall back into black.

Friday 16th January 1998

Today I can't win though, my gas is appalling, my stomach is in pain and bloating. The Colofac has just made things worse. I feel so uncomfortable with my body like this, my middle feels ugh.

Been here 8 weeks now. The atmosphere's been so down.

Sunday 18th January 1998

Am quite low this evening, just fed up of being here, all I do is eat and I'm sick of it at the moment. Same old routines, rules and so on and so on. Yet at least another 4 weeks to go. I want to go sooner but am I ready, really ready? After going out with Mum yesterday it's made me see that I am coping better than I thought I would so far. I'm impatient, uneasy or am I also scared of staying and pushing things that little bit further. If I was getting more out of the groups . . . I've buckled down to pushing the weight on, now I need some more practice with everyday living.

Tuesday 20th January 1998

Today, no this afternoon and definitely evening, have been a mess and chaotic, well not entirely chaotic. I did what I had to do otherwise I would have bounced off the walls and more than likely launched my fist through a pane. I've spent too long being doubted and labelled by others and in turn myself. I will not sit back and be told I'm anorexic and will be until I get over 85%. I'm fucking proud of how far I've come in the past few weeks despite being so damn ill, yet I can never do enough weight-wise for him and to be quite frank I'm sick of it. I am sure, am solid in myself, I believe and have proved I'm not anorexic.

I don't need official statistics to conform to, that's bollocks, it's the individual that counts and I'm strong. DAMN STRONG. I'm angry certainly because I feel insulted. I shouldn't let him wind me up but I offer honesty and I speak my own truth. It's all I offer up openly but it doesn't seem to count. I need a challenge, not for him to suggest I take putting on weight as a challenge, ha! It doesn't even come close, stressful maybe because I'm pushing and pushing myself but I'm reaching the limit. Physically I can do little more except stay in bed and only rise for food. Great life. So by the time I get to discharge I'll not have encountered the real challenges that lie outside, then I'm fucked basically. Every day I try to maximise input, it's more a chore, part of daily life, hardly challenging. There is more to me than just the body. I'm going to know more about weight by the time I leave than I ever did before!

I'm going to keep legging it, tonight was the graveyard but each time I'll get further and further. If I'm hemmed in I have to find my own way out. The problem is, if I wasn't so bloody sensible I'd discharge myself now but I know I'd fall at the first hurdle because reality seems so far away. That is why I need more behind me. If I go back to drink to cope I'll get physically ill and the pattern will begin of me moving further away to be ill alone and this time I'd disappear for good. Selfish, very selfish, but you and others remain unhappy either way.

Yet again tired and drained. Once more on obs and a loss of hope. The weeks seem endless and the time, the time barely moves so instead I'd rather have bed.

Thursday 22nd January 1998

Had a gorgeous massage last night, a whole hour of deep, intense hands on. It reminded me of how much I enjoy being touched and how it makes me feel. Wonderful.

Sunday 25th January 1998

Today there is an oddness inside I can't describe but it's a general sense of feeling unwell. So have spent the majority of the day in and out of toxic dreams and thoughts. All kinds of people and places have been in and out of my head, being with Ian, visiting Keswick, catching up with old friends, Felixstowe. Apart from all that this week on the whole has been grand, if all the weeks were this pleasant I could cope with the time more.

Since I'm at the 8 stone mark I've been doing a lot of thinking and looking. From here on in it's a new journey, the potential for growth, it's exciting. I like what I see, what I feel, yet I think I must have been under so much mental and emotional pressure and physical pain because to be honest 8 stone is nothing. I don't feel that different whereas 5 years ago that was the final straw I wasn't ready for or comfortable with, it's crazy. Maybe now because I feel healthier, mentally lighter, clearer and at ease. Also I have another half a stone to go and I'm not fearing flesh. It's all so strange. Even when I got my body back before it was nowhere as good as it is now. I remember my skin was all dry and my legs were mottled like salami, my stomach straining yet now there is strength, it's supple and I am beautiful, radiant.

Wednesday 28th January 1998
Dinner time still turns into a complete fiasco, they're like a bunch of whining old women at times. Physically been feeling quite bloated and my midriff feels very uncomfortable, it's strange. I feel generally in myself strange, strangely achy and balloon like.

THIS IS ALL SO BORING . . . END IT.

FEBRUARY
Monday 2nd February 1998
Things have not been right for days. I've been crying so much since Friday. I could barely talk without tears. It comes down to security and safety, the things I crave, and this is why I need them because they've not been here for years. Ian is the only . . . not the only but one of the few people I feel safe with, that's why staying with him after St Clements calmed me. I knew I was safe from harm. It sounds strange, even stupid but I have to find it again, find it within myself somehow. I wish it was there to return to . . .

Tuesday 3rd February 2998
Thoughts change so quickly, moods and emotions. Migraine brewing . . .

Thursday 5th February 1998

Stuffed beyond comfort. I can't take much more of this, my stomach and bowels aren't coping with the quantity at all and am in much discomfort and pain.

Monday 9th February 1998

Finally had home leave which went OK but it's made me see I have nothing to go back to, which I know sounds a bit harsh but in a lot of ways it's true. I'm just so fucking aimless. I'm not even sure if I'll stay at Mum's any more. Aaargh. Basically it's like, what the fuck am I going to do?

I could endlessly drift from place to place. See, I'm torn, torn between what's right and wrong for me, will I be chasing dreams? I can't wish for things to be different, wish for Cumbria to have lasted longer, I was too ill, I know that and nothing could have made a difference. Half of me needs some reason to settle, something solid, something sound even if it's not definite. When I think about this mess I just cry, cry because it's so empty, cry because I'm too weak to make a stand, make a commitment. I'm in running mode, get well and fuck off somewhere . . . which I can do but it's what I have been doing for years, just keep on moving further and further.

NOV, EMBER

I lie awake in the half light with wandering eyes
and a head full of sins with nowhere to begin
and the urge to run, to find someone
to live without the need for a knife.
KNIFED again
and I refrain from detailing pain,
to empty ears I'm recalling fears
that rewind and replay most everyday.
Snatched moments, lost words
that'll never be heard.
KNIFED again
bottle burning the skin, leaving scars.
I remove and replace
clutching, curling tightly in vain
but the tension remains.

Thursday 12th February 1998
Thoughts keep coming yet I don't write them, feelings remain uncaptured and lost. The news so far is that I'm now on a maintenance diet! So I'm on the final stretch.

My mind has been buzzing and on Tuesday it got so buggered I could barely haul myself out of bed and I hate it. Hate this scared sensation. Scared of commitment. Before I was scared of being accepted by the family and it was easier to remain apart rather than be accepted into something that wasn't me but now I've moved on to fear of commitment. I suppose it's because I just don't know what the right thing is to do first. I guess I don't want to get trapped either. There has to be a happy medium somewhere.

Enveloped

Sunday 15th February 1998
My head is quite buggered again, some of it is extreme tiredness, my eyes feel like slits. I just want to cry and cry really, it feels like there's a lot of pain welling, welling inside. I really am not in the mood for being stuck in here. I want air, I want light but instead I've a head so low that it's all such an effort.

VI-O-LEN-C

Cruel in body, cruel in mind
I was certainly never that kind,
the violence I craved came from within.
Spiteful words, a vicious tongue licked
'You're useless, pathetic
and don't count for shit.'
Battered. bruised, pale and blue,
lips bleeding and bitten from being so chewed.

Tired, pained and totally drained
I like inert, surrounded by dirt.
Head swimming, eyes skimming
the creases and folds of covers curled tight
while I pray for night
but even in sleep I still can't find peace.

Monday 16th February 1998
I see beauty staring back at me. Fabulous in flesh!

Tuesday 17th February 1998
My head is fucked by tiredness and feel very rundown. All day I've been in and out of toxic dreams, all quite hopeful, spent the afternoon in Keswick, reliving the summer and thoughts of love. Tired, irritable, head of lead and feel so lonely, I need to

be held and hear kind words. I'm not ready yet . . .

Sunday 22nd February 1998 – Dallinghoo
So far the weekend's gone well, aside from the fact I am in much physical pain, my bones and joints ache intensely. I'm just so tired and rundown that it hurts. It's crazy, I'm quite keen to get back to hospital so I can lie down but I know once I'm there I'll regret having dashed back. So . . . mask up and hang in there.

Sunday evening. I had to come back early in the end, so ill that all I could do was lie hugging a hot water bottle. Cried because I can't cope with the pain. The weekend has just been a failure really, just couldn't cope. I don't understand why I seem so exhausted so much. My life shouldn't be like this, ruled by tiredness. How will I manage when there's no safe sanctuary to return to?

Tonight I feel brighter though, very tearful, to be back amongst friends makes all the difference. I really don't mind another month or so, even longer as when I leave I'll really miss these girls. I know I've moaned about the mealtimes etc. but I'm with such lovely people I can talk to and understand. It means so much to me.

Tuesday 24th February 1998 – Dukes Priory Hospital
Yesterday was one fucked up day. The whole place is stressed; dinners are tense and tearful, it's crowding in. 11 of us and only 2 staff, we're not getting the care we need. In turn we mother the newer ones who don't believe.

Wednesday 25th February 1998
Sat at breakfast and wondered what it must be like to get up normally, to start off the day with a sense of being able to go and do whatever you wanted or needed to but instead I see the green

striped walls of the dining room. Part of me is fighting back now, the bit that knows I'm too scared of leaving. Another month is another month of tedium and safety, restraint that is making me low. I can't face another day like this.

Thursday 26th February 1998

Fucked would describe how yesterday turned out. Ended up getting sectioned because I confided how low I was feeling and my worries, then they think I'll do something impulsive and won't let me go on leave. I should learn to keep my mouth shut. If I can't be honest then what's the point anyway? I can't always pretend because the cracks appear eventually. Spent hours just crying and crying. I have truly had enough of being here, I don't need it any more, all it's doing is making me worse. Frustrating. Being sectioned just made me feel even worse about myself, that I've failed.

I can be sectioned like this yet even when I was actively suicidal last year, and before at 5st 10lbs and about to keel over dead several years ago, nothing was done when clearly that would have been an ideal situation. If I wasn't a danger to myself then I don't know what the fuck I was!

Saturday 28th February 1998

After fucking the majority of this week up, things are turning out alright now. I mean I still feel quite low but can't be helped, at least I got out for a couple of hours this afternoon. I've realised that give or take a few weeks the past 7 months have been spent in psychiatric wards, it's no wonder I'm feeling so caged and out of touch.

MARCH
Tuesday 3rd March 1998
Only slept vaguely last night, very lightly at times then not at all, with the slightest noise alerting me and I thought, I thought a lot, a lot of toxic, feverish sequences fading in and out. Hence I've slept pretty much through the morning.
The feeling of loving one sided is hard.

Thursday 5th March 1998 – Felixstowe
I wish I was going back to hospital tonight, it does my head in being there, yet after a day or two out I want to go back because I just don't cope so well. I have to make sure I keep busy when I'm discharged otherwise my life will be so fucking boring there will really be no point. That scares me, it really does. I don't want much out of life except some safety, love, you know the usual stuff, but walking along the beach I longed to be somewhere I really felt I belonged, somewhere I fitted in, with a background, an identity and value, yet I'm so lost.

Saturday 7th March 1998 – Dukes Priory Hospital
The majority of last night was spent awake and thinking, interspersed with moments of toxic sleep. The main problem seeming to be that I lack identity, I lack self confidence and this question of value . . . these are all core issues that need to be addressed quite intensely because otherwise I'll remain a lost soul. But how?

Friday 13th March 1998
A lot of crap has happened this week, most distressing of all has been the flare up between Mum and myself after a very harsh phone call. Her words cut very deep, so much so that I felt I'd had enough of the family and was preparing to make a total break but . . . it's not what I want, I just don't know any other

way to cope since I've been such a let down as a daughter. I've cried so much about all this and am back to square one without anywhere to return to at the moment so that now needs sorting.

Then a letter came today as well, at least I know where I stand, I think, it's not as though I don't realise she's had enough of it all and is just darn frustrated with my lack of direction, conviction and so on. It gets to me just as much too as I'm the one who should be changing things for the better. I'm a little stuck, that's all (understatement!).

Thursday 19th March 1998

Spent some of the day at Lakeside and went off with Bec. She really is a great girl and a good friend. I've been awake since 3.30 a.m. with a stonking head on, so by the time we got back I was aching and yucky. Thrush is back with a vengeance too. Have slept most of the evening drifting in and out of toxic thoughts about the future but all quite hopeful.

Despite everything I felt as though I can cope with what lies ahead.

APRIL

Tuesday 14th April 1998

Today I felt so strong, it's something to cling to and I know that my life will be shit if I just give up and let it be that way. Everyday, however small, I must make it work, even if it's gaining a simple joy.

Enveloped

What happened next? . . . still in Felixstowe (1999)

The diaries don't end there; they continue to record the problems of life beyond hospital although quite sporadically, becoming more concerned with detailing dreams that won't leave me.

Ten days after writing the final entry in what became *Enveloped*, I was discharged from hospital and returned to Felixstowe. I remember becoming increasingly fearful of my seeming lack of identity and purpose, as the prospect of everyday living scared me: the last time I had felt normality was many years ago. Having spent six months being looked after, I now suddenly had to try and effectively cope with day to day life and all it entailed. Along with that I still have the practicalities of coping with a food allergy (dairy products) and food intolerances (wheat, gluten, soya, eggs, yeast, sugars, excessive fats and certain fruits, vegetables and meats). Even on leaving hospital I was still physically weak, suffering from draining tiredness and limb pains. Gradually though I have managed to rebuild my strength but am only able to do a fraction of what others can as the fatigue is close and extreme.

The days, weeks and months following discharge were hard. Thankfully though, staying with Ian helped immensely; I have always known I am safe with him. He calmed me when I felt uneasy and confused which gave me the space to begin again.

In July 1998 I took the step of moving, one of my biggest tests; it was something I knew I had to do, it also filled me with dread. The thought of living in a room held the potential for isolation. However it provided the independence and sanctuary I craved yet feared.

I started writing that summer. It has become my outlet for expresion. All the unresolved pieces, past, present and potential, whirlpooled through poetry. I released words I could not speak.

Enveloped

Along with the acceptance and publication of *Tincture*, a small anthology of poetry, the excitement and achievement fuelled me.

In the autumn of '98 I began working part time, until May of this year, when my health forced me to make a decision. Remaining well takes priority and it's just a case of having to adjust life. After years of self-neglect I intend to do what I know is right, regardless. I take life at a slower pace which suits. Now I've settled there is no longer the need to run away from the nightmare that had been pursuing me, place after place.

I am still amazed by the enormous effects that allergies and intolerances continue to have on me. Foods were identified and excluded. The fog of despair that had surrounded me began to lift, although the physical symptoms took longer. The discovery has changed my life. How many others are misdiagnosed and could change their lives?

I continue to live on a restricted diet consisting mainly of chicken, potatoes, rice, carrots, broccoli, pears and peaches. I won't deny I've been tempted, a slice of bread or a glass of wine, but I know from previous experiments that an adverse reaction would be immediate. Life now is a fine balance.

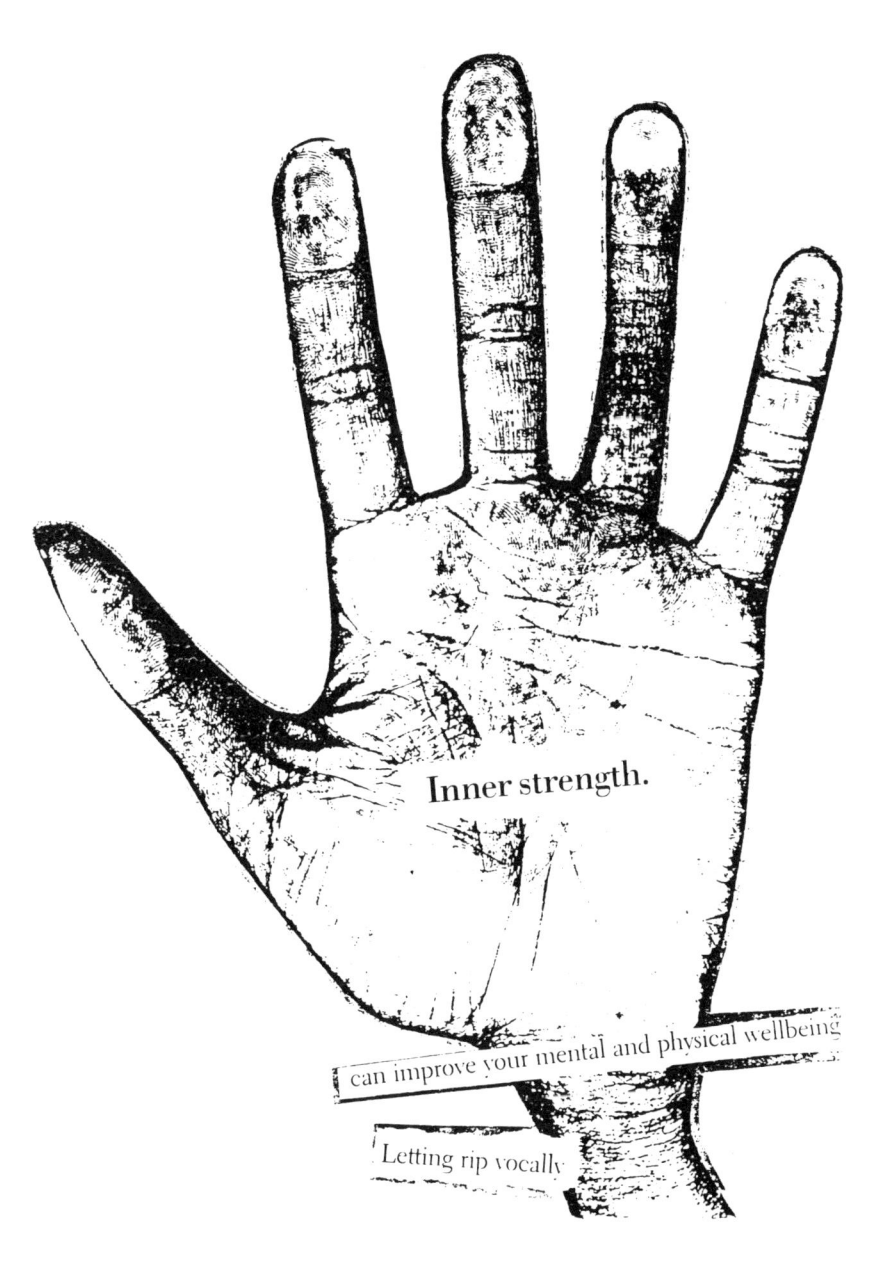

Inner strength.

can improve your mental and physical wellbeing

Letting rip vocally

Enveloped